Dear Young Programmer
Things I Wish You Knew

By **Brendan F. Hemingway**

Chief Technology Officer, Coyote Labs

First Edition (August 2018)

ISBN 978-1725198296 / 1725198290

Printed in the United States of America

Cow and Calf Publishing
5 Spring Road
Branford, CT 06405

This publication is designed to provide information in regard to the subject matter covered. It is sold with the understanding that the publisher and the author are not engaged to render legal, accounting or other professional services. If legal advice or other expert assistance is required, the services of a competent professional should be sought.

Table of Contents

Preface

Web Site (& Selfish Motivation)

There is a very simple web site which was put together to support this book and its URL is this:

http://coyote-labs.com/HSCS/

With that out of the way, let me be frank about why I wrote this book and why you should read it. A few paragraphs is all I ask. Then I will revert to official book author tone and no one has to know.

I am finally old enough to justify my natural surliness. At last my inside matches my outside. And my inside has something to say. Many things to say, actually, but all those things to say flow from this deceptively simple statement:

I have worked with many, many programmers over many years in many different settings. I ran into so many self-taught programmers; in the beginning of my career, the self-taught were mostly grad students who decided not to pursue physics, or law or medicine. As time went on, the other programmers got younger and younger and more and more of them were refugees from college itself. The new programmers were not only self-taught but self-taught by their middle school or high school selves and (brace yourself) it showed. Sometimes it really showed. I kept wishing that I were able to go back in time and have their early teen self self-teach them a few things that might not seem interesting or worthwhile. But these things are certainly worthwhile and might even be interesting. Them knowing these things might make my working life easier and better. Knowing these things will certainly make their working life easier and better.

While it is too late for many of the programmers I have worked with it is not too late for you, dear Reader, my future colleagues. Please, do us both a favor and give me a chance. Let me help you help me.

Introduction

This book is intended as an introduction to the concepts which are the building blocks of Computer Science (CS). As an introduction, this book is not an in-depth treatment of these concepts; rather it is a road map which you can use to go deeper on your own, as needed or desired.

This book is intended to give CS neophytes an idea of what CS covers and what problems CS solves.

What Is Computer Science?

Computer Science is the formal study of the areas which support Computer Programming.

The subset of CS I will introduce is this:

• Hardware

• Programming languages

• Data storage and retrieval

• Data structures

• Searching and sorting

• Client/Server interactions

• Networking

• Debugging

Why Study CS?

I was introduced to Computer Science (CS) just after I was introduced to Computer Programming. CS was a framework and a foundation for learning programming.

Starting with the basic concepts before trying to apply them is a natural series of events so I thought nothing of it. I assumed that all programmers would follow a similar path until I started meeting programmers who were never given any grounding in CS. I saw problems caused by the gaps in their knowledge and the time wasted by their lack of formal training, as they struggled to solve difficult problems which were solved decades ago.

Given that so many young people are already deeply familiar with computers by the time they reach high school, and since so many budding technologists have already spent hours programming without any formal training, this book presents CS in the context of programming.

My dream is an industry in in which all programmers are armed with a basic knowledge of the underlying concepts. With this basic knowledge, the programmer will know where to look for more information when one of these concepts is the answer to a vexing programming problem.

Your dream, I hope, is to be a well-rounded and effective programmer, either as an outstanding solo programmer or a well-regarded member of a team.

It is so much easier to learn good habits when you are young. It is so much easier to learn the background when you are learning the fun parts. Your future self will thank you.

No matter how talented you are, or how smart, or how dedicated, there are many problems with teaching yourself to program without learning very much about CS. The problem I find most concerning is the crippling disadvantage you will have when trying to debug complex technologies. In order to debug an issue with a complex technology, you need to break down that complex technology and understand it. In order to understand a complex technology, you have to comprehend more than one kind of technology. If you only know what you think you need to know and you only know about your own coding, there will be a vast array of issues you cannot debug.

This Book's Conventions

This section describes the conventions used in this book as an aid to navigating.

End of Chapter Exercises

Since this book is an introduction, you may want more detail than is provided. For those readers, every chapter ends with a "Delve Deeper" section which has suggestions for going into more detail on your own.

SA: Security Alerts

When a topic brings up a security issue that issue will be marked with "SA:" in front of the header, so you can find them in the index, and with this graphic in the text:

This is part of my crusade to have programmers think more about security.

History Lessons ☺

In writing this book I have come to face a painful truth: many of you don't know much about computing history because you do not find computing history very interesting.

I struggled to wrap my mind around this, even though it is somewhat obvious in hindsight. My enthusiasm for history and my deep belief that history provides insight meant that I have a blind spot where history is concerned. I assumed that young programmers were just unlucky not to have been exposed to history.

I had larded the text with many gens of computing history, confident that readers would be as delighted to encounter this as I would be. I was very wrong. Many of the pre-publication readers politely mentioned these asides, and never with enthusiasm.

However, I am as stubborn as computer programmers tend to be, so I am keeping the history asides but I have been convinced to make it easier to find (and, presumably, avoid) them by marking them with this graphic: ☺

In Praise of Abstraction

I love abstraction. I naturally gravitate toward abstraction as way of putting my mental arms around new concepts, or unfamiliar technology. I map out new things on paper. I diagram out problems and plans and ideas.

However, I have discovered that many other people do not share my love of abstraction. In particular, young men seem to prefer to hold all the details in their heads. People who do not share my love of abstraction often do not see the point of all the mapping and general overviews and the documentation and the diagrams.

More to the point, lots of young programmers like to roll up their sleeves and start right in; they do not tend to want to do any background reading, or elaborate planning, or writing of design documents.

All things being equal, this would just a difference without any way to resolve it, like Marvel vs DC or Star Trek vs Star Wars or iOS vs Android. But all things are not equal, for the following reasons:

1. Keeping things in your head is handy, but not a good way to work with other people.

2. Keeping things in your head is easier when you are younger, but you won't always be young; trust me on this.

3. Keeping things in your head is easier when there aren't many other things in your head; it has been about 40 years since I started programming and there are lots of things in my mental attic.

If you are the sort of programmer who wants to keep it all in your head, then you are in the Concrete camp. If you are in the Concrete camp, then think of Abstraction as a way of getting all the concrete details into your head once you have more concrete details than your head can hold.

As a bonus, when other people ask you what you are working on, or how far along you are, or how things are going, you can avoid one of the most dreaded fates of the Young Programmer: being labelled a tiresome bore who always gives too much detail. In place of all that detail you can roll out the abstraction.

Levels of Abstraction

CS often has to bridge the gap between the abstract and the concrete. For example, algorithms in this context are descriptions of how software should behave; algorithms are very abstract. But a computer running software written from that algorithm is quite concrete.

The levels from lowest to highest are these:

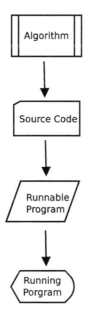

This the way I will be exploring the concepts.

Layered Architecture

The most common use I will make of the levels of abstraction is the "layered architecture" concept which I will to break down the architecture of technology into manageable chunks.

For people who prefer to get their technical information visually, rather than verbally, "block diagrams" are a great way to represent layered architectures. See the "Delve Deeper" section for more.

As a quick example of the layered architecture in action, let us consider the Cloud through this lens.

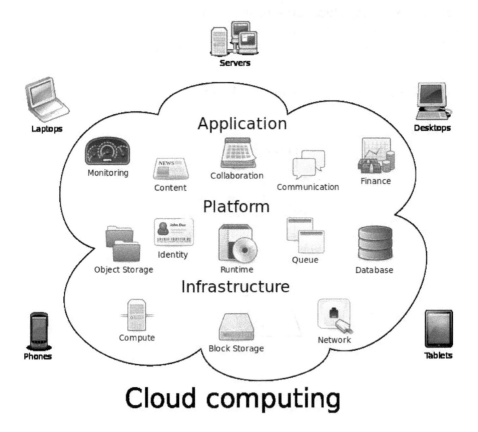

Cloud computing diagram By Sam Johnston [1]

LAYERS OF THE CLOUD

Here is a simplified layered architecture for the Cloud, using pulling up a web page from a server as our example:

1. A client computer runs a browser which allows the user to follow a link to get a web page.

2. A message is sent over a network from the client to the server specified in the link.

3. A server computer which accepts the request, finds the requested web page and then sends the web page back to the client.

4. The client renders the web page so the user can see it.

Variable Focus

Note that the level of detail in the layered architecture varies as needed. A large part of the benefit of using the layered architecture is being able to use the level of detail needed to examine the question at hand. You can always zoom in by looking at particular layer's layers. This is less complicated than it may seem as will be demonstrated below.

Details Do Not Matter, Until They Do

Abstraction is powerful because it lets us make simplifying assumptions. For instance, we have the abstraction of a 'file' which lets us store data on a persistent storage device, without having to actually know if the device is a hard drive, a USB stick, a CD-ROM disc or paper tape. The abstraction links a file name to its contents and we do not have to worry about the concrete details.

Abstraction is useful because it trims the scope of our work. To continue with the file example, this abstraction allows us to not worry about the details of the persistent storage device. We can just assume that we can read from and write data to the file.

Abstraction is also subject to failure and its failure mode is not graceful. When it breaks, it shatters. Glass is very strong until it fails and when it fails it shatters. Gold is not very strong but as you put gold under stress it deforms quite a bit before it breaks. Glass is brittle; gold is ductile. Abstractions, especially in CS, tend to be very brittle.

Consider the abstraction of "the file." The abstraction associates a name with some data. You can create files, rename them and delete them. You can open a file to gain access to the data. Once the file is open, you have a handle from which you can read to get data from the file (if you opened it for reading). Or you can write to the file through the handle if you opened for writing. You can close a file handle which ends your access.

Consider common ways in which this abstraction fails. If some other user deletes the file while you are reading from it, what happens? There is no obvious response given the abstraction. [2] If you run out of space on the disk while you are writing to it, what happens? That is also not very clear from the abstraction. [3]

So abstraction hides things from us so those things do not matter--until they do.

Context Is Always Important

As in so many things in human interactions, context matters.

My favorite example of this comes from sociology: a sociologist was studying interactions between co-workers and came across the following illustration of how important context can be:

An employee comes into the office and is greeted by another employee who says "Wow, you look awful!". In the first instance, the speaker is a friend and the reply is "Oh, I know, our kid is teething and we were up all night." In the second instance, the speaker is not a friend and the reply is an angry scowl.

To the observer, the two scenarios are different only in the reply. This difference is only explained by context and is inexplicable without context. Context can be subtle, context can be invisible, but it is always important.

In computing we often refer to context as "the defaults" and in computing the answer to questions is often "context." The default behavior of software is often determined by configuration files. The defaults often provide the context of the user experience. When a user users a command line interface, such as the DOS box in Windows or the shell in Unix systems, the current working directory is the context for file names. You can change that context by changing directory or by using absolute path names. (Don't worry if this does not make sense, all will be made clear when we examine file systems in a later chapter on Operating Systems.)

Thrown By The Hardware Curve

As a result of over-reliance on abstraction and dependance on excess hardware power, lots of software is written without a thought to careful use of hardware resources. This is all just fine until it isn't: sometimes the software's performance just sucks and then many programmers have nothing to fall back on. Just as debugging requires an ability to see the forest for the trees, so does finding and fixing performance bottlenecks.

☺ Over the several decades of my various careers in computer programming, Moore's Law has come the rescue of many bad programmers writing mediocre, inefficient software. We call this "riding the hardware curve."

"Moore's Law" is named for Gordon Moore, a legend of the early CPU business. In 1965, he predicted that CPU speed would increase geometrically for at least the next decade and he was right. For those of us who starting using computers in the 1970s, Moore's Law became shorthand for the rapid growth of the computer power [4] in general and CPU speed in particular.

To be fair, there are plenty of working programmers who disagree with me on this, who feel that as long as computers become more capable and environments offer more features, time spent worry about efficiency is time wasted. ☺

Delve Deeper, Chapter 1

1. Read more about Gordon Moore and his "law"; Wikipedia is a great place to start.

2. Figure out how much more powerful computers are since you were born.

3. Research block diagrams; Wikipedia is a good resource here but not the only one.

4. Create a layered architecture for your favorite piece of computer technology, both verbally and as a block diagram.

Chapter 1 End Notes

[1] Created by Sam Johnston using OmniGroup's OmniGraffle and Inkscape (includes Computer.svg by Sasa Stefanovic)This vector image was created with Inkscape., CC BY-SA 3.0, https://commons.wikimedia.org/w/index.php?curid=6080417

[2] What actually happens is O/S-dependent.

[3] What usually happens in this case you get an I/O error and you do whatever you think you should do.

[4] The concept of computer power and a working definition will come up in a later chapter.

Hardware Resources

One framework for considering programming is that programming is about controlling resources in a computer environment. At the lowest level, that enviroment's resources the hardware.

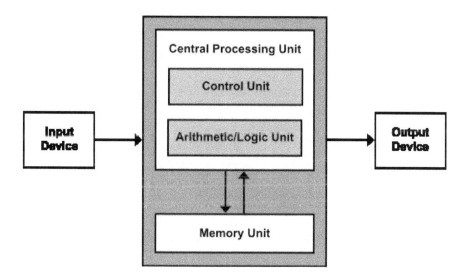

Hardware block diagram, see Wikipedia entry for "Computer hardware"

Running Program (Hardware)

I will often start our explorations of various CS concepts using the running program as the jumping off point. The running program is usually the most basic concept we have of using a computer, at least as programmers.

A running program is a package of hardware instructions for the Central Processing Unit or "CPU", commonly called "the processor."

Before the CPU can "see" those instructions they have to be loaded into Random Access Memory or "RAM", commonly called "the memory."

The instructions, or "Machine code", are understood by the CPU; indeed, they are all the CPU can understand. In the usual case, the instructions were loaded from a file which came from persistent storage-- a rather academic term for the mass storage device in a computer, much more commonly called "the hard disk" or "the hard drive."

Classic Software Model

The classic running program model is this:

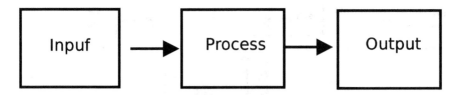

Input generally comes from input devices such as keyboards or "Network Interface Cards" or "NIC" and is the hardware which connects the host computer to the network.

Processing is done by the CPU and other processors such as a floating point processor (FPU).

Output generally comes out of output devices such as printers, monitors and NICs.

Common Hardware

That simple description touches on the following hardware:

• CPU

• RAM

• Storage

- Keyboards

- NICs

- Printers

- Monitors

Biological Analogy

When I was starting out, cognitive scientists actively resisted the tendency of CS folks to use the human brain as an analogy to computer hardware. But over time, the analogy has been embraced even to point where some people call the brain's thinking patterns "wetware." The "wet" comes from the tendency of living tissue to be wet and "ware" by analogy with software and hardware (and middleware and firmware: man do we lack imagination for CS terminology). Yuck.

Here is the brain analogy:

- The CPU is the "thinking part" of the brain, the thing that runs the mind

- The RAM is the short-term memory in which the brain stores recent events before storing those memories in long-term memory.

- The persistent storage is the long-term memory: slower and harder to access but longer-lasting.

- The keyboards and scanners and cameras are the eyes and ears: not part of the brain but directly connected to the brain.

- The printers and monitors are the voice and handwriting which are the ways in which the brain can transfer information to other brains.

CPU

The CPU is a collection of electrical circuits which execute instructions. As will be covered in the chapter on Machine Code, these instructions are generally very simple. Just as brick structures can be varied and complex even though they are made up simple, regular bricks, so complex software can be made out of very simple instructions. Many, many simple instructions. So many instructions.

CPUs execute instructions by switching between various pathways through a network of switches. In this context the switches act as gates to direct the flow of control through the possible gates to end up in different parts of the collection of switches.

For those of us who are not electrical engineers and not physicists and not interested in solid-state electronics there is a terrific model for how CPUs work: The Billiard-ball Computer. Wikipedia's entry on the Billiard-ball Computer is a good starting point.

VACUUM TUBES

The original CPUs were built from vacuum tubes. Vacuum tubes were invented in 1904 and eventually enabled the first generation of what we call "electronics." One of these electronic devices was the early versions of what we now call "computers." (Another of these electrical devices was the original CRT TV set and the CRT-based computer monitors.)

But vacuum tubes were relatively slow and relatively inefficient electrically which meant that they got pretty hot pretty quickly and tended to burn out on a regular basis.

TRANSISTORS

The CPU was revolutionized by the advent of the transistor; the transistor is much smaller, quicker switch than the vacuum tube.

Much smaller means more gates in the CPU which means more complex instructions and more instructions.

Quicker switching means more instructions executed per second which means a faster CPU and better computer performance.

REGISTERS

CPUs are circuits on a circuit board. The only way into or out of a circuit board are the connectors wired into the circuit.

At the abstract level, we say that the CPU has a special relationship with particular chunks of memory called "registers." Registers are chunks of RAM that the CPU can access directly. The rest of the memory is what we usually mean by RAM and RAM is only accessible to the CPU "indirectly." By "indirectly" we mean that the CPU has to first execute some instruction which copies from RAM into the register.

At the concrete level, the CPU is wired into the CPU's circuitry. This means that the CPU can access the registers directly, without an intervening instruction. Each wire is part of a circuit and each wire either has charge or not. Thus each wire has two states: charged, which we call "on" or "one" and no charge, which we call "off" or "zero." This wired connection means that the CPU's connection to registers is on a wire-by-wire basis, creating a string of bits (see below) which can either be 1 or 0.

In other words, at a deep level, the computer is an electrical appliance for creating and manipulating numbers which are expressed as lists of bits, which we will call "bitstrings."

Bitstrings may seem like a rather spare notation. Bitstrings may not seem like a particularly useful way to represent numbers, let alone add, subtract, divide or multiply numbers. Bitstrings certainly do not seem like a powerful way for the CPU to communicate with other hardware.

Things are not always as they seem: bitstrings are surprisingly powerful and surprisingly useful and, if you write software which interacts directly with hardware, probably unavoidable.

Luckily, there is an entire branch of mathematics which is devoted entirely to bitstrings and the rules which govern them. Luckily, someone went to the very great effort of creating a formal description of how one handles bitstrings. Luckily, there is Boolean Algebra.

BOOLEAN ALGEBRA

Boolean Algebra is math with Base 2 numbers and so is sometimes called "binary math." Since "binary" can refer to a particular kind of data as well as a particular kind of math, I try to stick with "Boolean" for the math and "binary" for the data.

Boolean Algebra was defined by a British mathematician named George Boole in 1847, a very long time before the modern electronic computer was ever imagined.

Boolean algebra started life as a glorious abstraction: what is the absolute minimal number system which would still be a complete number system? This lead Boole to another question: what if you did algebra with only two digits: 0 and 1? Because each digit has only two options, they are said to be *bi*nary dig*its*, or "bits" for short.

We call Boolean numbers "bitstrings" because they are strings of bits.

When decoding bitstrings, each bit can be either 0 or 1 but the value is the 2 to the power of the digit. For handy reference, let us review the powers of 2 from 0 through 7.

```
Bit 0:    1
Bit 1:    2
Bit 2:    4
Bit 3:    8
Bit 4:   16
Bit 5:   32
Bit 6:   64
Bit 7:  128
```

To demonstrate bits as numbers, let us add 4 to 10:

```
00000100          4 in decimal (base 10)
00001010          10 in decimal (base 10)
--------
00001110          2 + 4 + 8 = 14
```

Or we could subtract 3 from 7:

```
00000111          7 in decimal
00000011          3 in decimal
--------
00000100          4 in decimal
```

Bits, as an abstraction, map perfectly onto the logical concepts of "true" and "false" which means that Boolean Algebra allows for a formal treatment of logical relationships. This property will be reviewed in more detail under the Boolean Algebra rubric in the Logic chapter.

Bits, as an abstraction, also map beautifully onto the electrical engineering's ability to detect the absence or presence of charge. No charge is zero, presence of charge is one; circuit off is zero, circuit on is one. Which means that electrical circuits can pretty easily do math so long as that math is in binary digits. The only options are these when doing math with a lefthand bit and a righthand bit.

```
+------+-------+-----+----------+
| Left | Right | Add | Subtract |
+------+-------+-----+----------+
|   0  |    0  |  0  |       0  |
+------+-------+-----+----------+
|   1  |    0  |  1  |       1  |
+------+-------+-----+----------+
|   1  |    1  |  2  |       0  |
+------+-------+-----+----------+
```

In the computer hardware context, bits come in packages of eight which we call "bytes" and which mean other languages call "octets." In Boolean algebra terms, a byte can be represented at a bitstring which is eight bits long. We number the bits from right to left, starting with zero and ending at seven.

So consider the bitstring "01101010":

```
+---+---+---+---+---+---+---+---+
| 7 | 6 | 5 | 4 | 3 | 2 | 1 | 0 |
+---+---+---+---+---+---+---+---+
| 0 | 1 | 1 | 0 | 1 | 0 | 1 | 0 |
+---+---+---+---+---+---+---+---+
```

Remember that any number raised to the power of 0 is 1. We write {number} to the power of X is written {number}^X. So ten to the power of zero is written "10^0" and equals 1.

```
Bit 0: bit is 0 x 2^0 =    0
Bit 1: bit is 1 x 2^1 =    2
Bit 2: bit is 0 x 2^2 =    0
Bit 3: bit is 1 x 2^3 =    8
Bit 4: bit is 0 x 2^4 =    0
Bit 5: bit is 1 x 2^5 =   32
Bit 6: bit is 1 x 2^6 =   64
Bit 7: bit is 0 x 2^7 =    0
                          ---
                          106
```

SIGNED / UNSIGNED

Bit 0 is often called "the Least Significant Bit" or LSB. Bit 0 is sometimes call "the low bit."

The highest bit in any byte, bit 7, is sometimes called "the Most Significant Bit" (MSB) or "the high bit." In the concrete case of computer memory and registers, the high bit is called "the sign bit" which raises the issue of representing negative numbers.

(What about multi-byte quantities? That is a topic for another chapter.)

There will a deeper dive into negative numbers in the Machine Code chapter, but for now a very basic explanation will suffice. In some contexts (there's that word again), we reserve the high bit to represent the sign of the quantity being represented. If the quantity is "unsigned" then the high bit is just another digit. If the quantity is "signed" then the high bit is a flag:

• 0 means no minus sign (i.e. a quantity greater than zero)

• 1 means a minus sign (i.e. a quantity less than zero)

But only context can determine whether or not the MSB is a sign bit or a value bit. There is no way know without knowing.

DECIMAL PLACES

The mathematically-inclined or more experienced reader may also wonder about decimal points. As with signed and unsigned values, this topic will be covered in detail that same later chapter. But for now, let us say that, natively, CPUs can only do binary *integers* (also called *whole numbers*). Implied decimal points and floating decimal points will also be covered later.

RAM

RAM stands for "Random Access Memory."

SAM ☺

The alternative to RMA is SAM, or "Sequential Access Memory." RAM was better in that one could access an element of it in one step. For this discussion, consider the byte to be the element of RAM.

SAM can only be accessed in sequence, just like folded sweaters in a drawer. To get to the sweater at the bottom of the drawer, you have to move each of the sweaters on top of that bottom sweater. Many hard disks (see below) are sequential devices.

RAM can be accessed in any sequence, just like folded sweaters laid out on a display table. You can see all the sweaters at once and grab whichever one you want.

(In fact, this is a good metaphor for many common programming tasks: loading your data off of disk and into RAM is very like unloading a drawer of its sweaters and laying them out on a table for easier access.)

The Cool Part of RAM

The cool part of RAM is the Random Access part, which supports the abstraction of arrays.

A traditional two dimensional array has rows and columns, so any element of a two dimensional array can be reached with a row index and a column index.

A one dimensional array is a single row of a two dimensional array so you do not need the row index because it is all the same row, you just need a column index. You only need one index. That makes the one dimensional array is a great abstract model for RAM because any element of an array can be accessed in one step via its index.

Hard Disks, aka Hard Drives

Hard disk were so named to distinguish them from floppy disks. "Hard drive" is another common name of the archetypal mass storage device. Originally a "magnetic drum" technology, now there are many common alternatives to the classic magnetic drum but we still call these devices "hard drives" or "hard disks."

Hard disks are still with us but floppies are just about extinct so we often just say "disk" or "drive."

Mass storage devices are generally large (lots of capacity), slow to access and cheap on a per unit basis.

An idea we want to introduce for later review is this: while both are, abstractly, a collection of bytes there are profound differences in the way we use RAM versus the way we mass storage. The fact that RAM is fast, but relatively expensive and relatively scarce means that we cannot naively slam data into RAM in order to process that data. There is very rarely enough RAM to hold all our data.

On the other hand, the fact that mass storage is slow but relatively cheap and relatively plentiful means that we can user more elaborate data structures to both speed up access and ease the effort of access. This rather vague assertion will become much cleared down the road, in a more detailed context.

Input and Output (I/O)

While Input and Output seem to be very different processes, in fact the hardware model is the same for both. This is so truc that computer systems often lumps them together into the same concept which we call "I/O."

That model is an abstraction. Sometimes an abstraction hides details and simplifies a complex situation. Sometimes an abstraction joins two dissimilar things. In this case the model is an abstraction that is both:

• The input device does whatever it does to acquire input which I will call "the data";

• The data ends up in a chunk of RAM called a buffer;

• The input device signals to the CPU [1] ;

• The CPU then can read from the buffer as it can read from any other RAM location;

So the model is this: wait for the signal, read from RAM. Repeat as needed.

Note that this model protects the CPU from having to know the details of how the input device works. Any input device--keyboards, USB sticks, paper tape readers, whatever--looks essentially the same to the CPU. Any input device which follows this model will work.

This is equally true of output: the CPU writes the data to be output into a RAM location and signals the output hardware that there is new data to write. The output device then does whatever it does to generate output: print on paper, write on a compact disc, whatever.

The I/O model is something of a specialty and the software which implements that model is called "a device driver." Drivers are part of Operating Systems so I will examine them in greater detail in the chapter on Operating Systems.

Delve Deeper, Chapter 2

1. Research Vacuum Tubes: how they worked, how quickly they could switch from one state to another. What CPUs were built with them? How fast could they execute instructions?

2. Research Transistors: how they work, how quickly they can switch from one state to another? How many transistors are in the typical modern CPU?

3. Learn more about George Boole and Boolean Algebra.

4. Express your age as a bitstring. (You will have to use your age in years as a whole number because our bitstring model cannot handle anything else.) How long is that bitstring? How many bytes would be needed to represent that bitstring?

5. Review the definition of integers.

6. Research "mantissa" and "exponent."

7. Compare and contrast floppy drives and hard drives.

Chapter 2 End Notes

[1] These signals are usually called thing so I will introduce them in that chapter.

Machine Code

Now that we know about the basic nature of the CPU, its relationship with its registers and the Boolean nature of those registers, I
am ready to tackle what the CPU does.

Running Program (Machine Code)

Let us return to our usual starting point, a running program.

In this context, machine code, a running program is a package of
instructions for the CPU which has been loaded into RAM to become a running process.

In this context I will ignore the role of the Operating System in
turning that package of instructions into a process and I will hand
wave the entire topic of I/O. I have good reason to ignore the Operating System (O/S for short) (see below).

P8B

In this chapter I will focus on the machine code itself. To do that, I
will image a particular CPU which never existed: the Puny 8 bit
Processor, or P8B for short.

Let us imagine the P8B as a very simple CPU:

• The P8B is an 8 bit processor, which means that its "word size"
  is one byte (8 bits). This means that its register are one byte big.
  It can handle one byte at a time.

• The PB8 has a very simple instruction set because all I want the
  P8B to be able to do is demonstrate how CPUs work.

• The P8B, as an 8 bit processor, can specify 256 (the maximum
  unsigned value of a byte) RAM locations which are numbered 0
  to 255. So the P8B's "addressable space" is 256 bytes.

• The P8B is register-based and has two registers which I call register 1 (R1) and register 2 (R2).

Assembler

At the dawn of (computer) time, values were entered into a computer via physical switches, each of which corresponded to a bit in a register (!). This process was on the way out when I started in computers. I was too cool to "toggle" instructions into a computer, but older programmers sneered at us kids who could load programs into computers via paper tape. Good times!

Then came assemblers, which were software tools to assemble runable packages from source files. Hurray! Software writing was born. Some people called writing software in machine code "assembler programming" and the software "assembly" and the people who did this work "assembly programmers."

MACRO ASSEMBLERS

Shortly after assemblers were invented, macro assembly was invented and macro assemblers were born. In the computing context, "macro" usually means "expanding a keyword into a longer or more specific format." Word processing macros help users write documents by expanding "#me#" to my name and title, or "#signature#" to my email signature.

In the assembly context, "macro" means "turning the mnemonic into the op code." The mnemonic code is a non-numeric name for an instruction which is easier for the programmer to remember and read and write. In the pre-GUI era, when we were using dumb ASCII terminals, computers were slow and typing was a pain and displays were small and ugly. So the mnemonics were generally three or four characters long and uppercase (some environments only supported uppercase, so uppercase was the safer choice. We weren't shouting all the time. We were just using uppercase.)

That service is needed to deal with the following issue. Consider the following bitstrings:

```
Bits      Value  Description
00000001  1      The number after zero and before two
00000001  1      Op code for SET (see below)
00000001  1      Op code designation for R1
```

⚠ You probably immediately noticed that the bitstring and the value are both the same in all three cases. So how do you know which is which? Context is how you know. This has important security implications which I will explore below, so I will repeat it: there is no way to know if a particular register value is an instruction, or data or parameter to an instruction. Context is the only way to know and context is not 100% reliable. ⚠

P8B Instruction Set

Here is the P8B instrument I will be working with now, although I may revise it later to make other points.

```
Op       Mne-
Code     monic   Description
----     -----   -----------
0        NOP     No operation
1        SET     Set a register's value
2        GET     Get a register's value
3        LOAD    Load a value from RAM
4        STOR    Store a value into RAM
5        ADD     Add R1 to R2
6        SUB     Subtract R1 from R2
```

NO-OPS

What is a NOP? It is a "no operation" or "no op". It is an instruction which does nothing. This does not sound very useful, but it is:

• No-ops provide a target for debuggers (break points) without interfering with the program's execution.

- No-ops provide padding so the program is easier to copy around (not a considering on a one byte machine, but when the time comes to consider two byte machines, or four or eight bytes the concept of "alignment" will make sense.)

- No-ops allow for patching existing executables without having to re-assembler or re-compile.

A side note on no-ops: if your machine code program reads a round number of bytes from a specific location, and the target data is smaller than you expect, the most likely result will be having your data padded at the end with binary zeroes. Which, surprise! I have defined as a no-op. And the people who designed the Z80 (see below) made the same choice.

In fact, there is no processor instruction set I have ever encountered where binary zero was not a no-op. If binary zero is a no-op then there is no harm done if machine code is padded out with binary zeroes. In our current context, there is no harm done if the boot loader requests a fixed number of bytes which is padded out with zeroes because the boot program does not exactly fill the MBR (or whatever the O/S called the on-disk structure which holds its boot program).

Op code Syntax

In the programming language chapter I will cover syntax (as opposed to grammar) and formal languages (as opposed to natural languages) but for now I will introduce a simple format for giving syntax.

Elements which are required will be given in braces, {like this}. Elements which are optional will be given in square brackets, [like this].

When there are options for an element, they are listed by | characters, like this: [apple | orange].

P8B ASSEMBLER SYNTAX

```
Op       Mne-
Code     monic    Parameters
----     -----    ----------
0        NOP
1        SET      {register} {value}
2        GET      {register} {values}
3        LOAD     {register} {address}
4        STOR     {register} {address}
5        ADD
6        SUB
```

P8B ASSEMBLER PARAMETERS

```
Op       Mne-
Code     monic    Options
----     -----    ----------
0        NOP
1        SET      {1 | 2} {0-255}
2        GET      {1 | 2} {0-255}
3        LOAD     {1 | 2} {0-255}
4        STOR     {1 | 2} {0-255}
5        ADD
6        SUB
```

FASM

Back in the days when four characters was plenty and uppercase was the norm, assembler was designated as "ASM"; in fact, Microsoft's macro assembler was called MASM. We often used "asm" as the file extension and assembler programs were often called ASM or some variant thereof.

Since I am making up P8B, I figured I would make up a macro assembler to help me write P8B programs. Because this macro assembler is, in some sense, "faux" I named it FASM.

FASM takes P8B assembler as input and gives a compiled P8B machine code program as output.

Real assemblers tended to be brutally simple because they were written in machine code. The heavy lifting of writing software was left to the human programmer so that the software was relieved of as much of the burden as possible.

In keeping with that spirit, FASM is pretty simple as well. The one indulgence I allowed myself is the line comment. I chose the semi-colon character for old time's sake.

FASM Input: prog1.asm

The FASM source code for our first program is provided in a listing in Appendix A. The listings and outputs are in an Appendix to keep from cluttering up the chapter but do not skip actually reading it, even if you have to flip to the back of the book to do it.

Behold the pain of assembler: you move in tiny steps and it takes so many lines to *do* anything. But consider the power of assembler: blazingly fast execution and no excess instructions. You also get total control of registers and bits which is often important in handling hardware.

TEXT VERSUS BINARY DATA

Before understanding the FASM's processing, I have to take a quick detour to a subject in some detail: text versus binary data.

So CPUs can only understand bitstrings. From bitstrings on can make numbers. But how do on make text?

The short answer is the now-familiar one: context. on cannot make text. on can only map numbers onto text, assuming that on knows that the numbers one is seeing are actually text.

The first such scheme to map numbers to letters was ASCII: the American Standard Code for Information Interchange. ASCII maps numeric values onto letters, numbers or punctuation. There are also "control characters" which control how text is displayed: tabs, carriage returns, line feeds, etc.

ASCII has some nifty properties:

- The MSB is not used, so ASCII values are only 7-bit and range up to 127.

- Uppercase and lowercase letter are 32 values apart, which is a bit, so moving between cases is really easy.

- ASCII encodes digits, which can be confusing; the digit nine is 57 in ASCII.

Let us consider bitstrings for the digit nine:

```
00001001        Binary value for 9
00111001        Binary value for 57, '9' ASCII
```

How do you know that 00111001 is not 57 but rather the digit nine? We don't; you have to rely on context.

Converting ASCII to binary is the reverse: you see 57 but you output 9.

FASM ASSEMBLER PROCESS

What does the FASM Assembler do with its input? Well, there are some very simplifying assumptions when processing P8B assembler:

1. Discard all the comments

2. Discard all blank lines after removal of comments

3. Each non-blank line results in a byte of output

4. If the line matches a macro keyword, output the op code

5. If the line matches an arabic number, output the binary value
ue

PROGRAM COUNTER

A package of executable code is executed from RAM. RAM's various locations can be accessed directly by address. The RAM's location addresses can be thought of as indices into an array. If you add one to the index, you get the next instruction. If you subtract one from the index, you get the previous instruction. The current index into the executable in RAM is call "the Program Counter" or PC. When the Personal Computer came along, things got confusing for a while.

Our program execution model is this:

• Load a machine code program into memory

• Point CPU at that memory

• Let the CPU march through that memory, using the PC as our index

THREADS

This model allows us to explain a computing construct called "threads." A thread is essentially allowing a second (or third or fourth or whatever) PC to run through the same program.

In theory, this allows for the apparent near-zero overhead of running a second (or third or fourth) copy of the program. In other words, once the first copy of the program is running, starting up other copies of it is very fast.

Web servers are an example of this in practice. Often, multiple threads are used to dramatically improve the performance of web servers. Giving each incoming connect its own thread through the web server is extremely quick and a light load on the hardware server. This allows relatively modest hardware to support relatively high numbers of connections as a web server.

Running "mult-threaded" software allows incoming connection to get the attention of an almost copy of the web server almost instantly, without the overhead of loading the machine code into memory and then pointing the CPU at it.

Notice the hedging: "apparent near-zero overhead" and "almost copy of the web server." The hedging is over some implementation details. In order to be mult-threaded, a program has to be "thread safe." In order to explain thread safety, I have to add a dimension to our model of a running program: instructions versus data.

INSTRUCTIONS & DATA

So far, we have not really thought much about it, programs are made up of two different kinds of data: instructions and data. Since you know that binary data is binary date, you know that the only difference between instructions and data is context. And that context is determined in no small part by the PC.

In CS we are rather stingy with the our letters and words. We often refer to instructions and data in the executing program context as "I&D."

SEPARATE I&D

```
┌─────────────────┐
│  Instructions   │
├─────────────────┤
│      Data       │
└─────────────────┘
```

Some computer architectures have separate I&D, by which we mean that the instructions are in one RAM chunk and the data is in another. Separate I&D means for much easer to be thread safe: your thread is a separate PC in the common instruction space, but you get your own copy of the data space. This increases overhead slightly because a new data space is allocated and initialized whenever a new thread is created. Separate I&D gives you slightly worse performance and much greater safety, which is a trade-off that is excellent for many tasks.

(Separate I&D is a great idea unless your app was created to be multi-threaded and the threads are not on a per-user basis but rather to create a family of related processes. In that case, the software designer may assume a mixed I&D environment and may further assume that they can use that shared memory to allow threads to communicate and coordinate their actions.)

MIXED I&D

```
Instructions
Data
Instructions
Data
Data
Instructions
```

Some computer architectures, like my imaginary P8B, have "mixed I&D" which means that instructions are combined in the program's runable image. Mixed I&D is much simpler to implement and therefore, in theory, more likely to be robust. But that simplicity also has some drawbacks. This will be come clearer through examining one of them.

SA: Buffer Overflow

In the mixed I&D environment, there is a pretty simple way to corrupt the PC: the buffer overflow attack.

The attack is easy to explain in the abstract: malicious software attacks an app by asking the app to put more data into a buffer than the buffer can hold. If the app does not do "bounds checking" (i.e. making sure that buffer size limits are not violated), then the buffer "overflows." In practice this means that the instructions which come after the end of the buffer will be overwritten. So when the PC jumps over the buffer to its "end" the PC will, in fact, be executing whatever the malicious software wants it to.

Buffer overflow attacks, like code injection attacks, are a symptom of sloppy programming and poor software engineering. Code you write should not have these vulnerabilities; it is relatively easy to avoid almost all of these vulnerabilities if you are a well-informed and conscientious programmer. You can do better and you should.

Variables

A variable is a name associated with a memory location. A variable has the following attributes:

1. A unique name, which has to meet some criteria: the name must not collide with reserved words, commands, etc. Names also cannot start with a digit, because that would make them look like numeric constant.

2. An offset into the memory block (more later); this is the FASM location.

3. A length, which in the FASM context is always one.

4. A data type, which in the FASM context is always "byte." There are many others, but I will bring them up later for a more complete treatment.

P8B ASSEMBLER OUTPUT

This is the output of the P8B assembler when it runs on prog1:

```
P8B (Puny 8 Bit Processor) app
P8B Assembler  in: prog1.asm
P8B Assembler out: prog1.p8b 27 bytes done.
```

This is a byte dump of the machine code.

Offset	Value	Offset	Value	Offset	Value
0	001	9	000	18	002
1	001	10	001	19	001

2	004	11	001	20	003
3	001	12	010	21	001
4	002	13	001	22	001
5	009	14	002	23	003
6	005	15	002	24	002
7	004	16	005	25	000
8	002	17	004	26	006

Not very informative, is it? That is why disassemblers were invented. A disassembler is just what it sounds like: a program which takes machine code as input and gives assembler source as output. Looking at disassembler output gives us a sense of what is lost in the assembly process.

So if there were a P8B disassembler, and it were run on the machine code for prog1, what would its output look like? To find out, I added disassembly to the P8B suite which is also in Appendix A.

This is much easier to read that a straight byte dump, but the comments and the whitespace are gone.

PROG1

In order to dip my toe into the macro assembler waters, I wrote a program to evaluate the following expression:

```
(4 + 9) - (10 + 2)
```

The final answer should be 1.

EMULATOR

When we say "emulator" in the computer programming context, we mean software which takes the place of some hardware.

Since the P8B hardware never existed, I could not find one on which to run FASM software. That is not a problem, because I wrote software to do what the P8B hardware would do, if it existed. So I can act as if the P8B existed, because I have a P8B emulator.

P8B RUNNING PROG1

I used my P8B emulator to run the machine code version of prog1. My emulator gives a status report after every instruction because why not? The output gives me confidence that the emulator is working and gives you a step-by-step record of what happened.

The first column of the emulator output is the PC; the rest of the columns are labeled.

Note that the PC always goes up, but not in simple increments because sometimes the PC is bumped up to account for the arguments to an instruction. This is a mixed I&D architecture, after all.

The last column is the PC after executing the current instruction.

```
P8B (Puny 8 Bit Processor) app
P8B Emulator...input file: prog1.p8b...27 bytes of program

[  0] Op Code: 1 (SET ) R1:    4 R2:    0
[  3] Op Code: 1 (SET ) R1:    4 R2:    9
[  6] Op Code: 5 (ADD ) R1:    4 R2:   13
[  7] Op Code: 4 (STOR) R1:    4 R2:   13
[ 10] Op Code: 1 (SET ) R1:   10 R2:   13
[ 13] Op Code: 1 (SET ) R1:   10 R2:    2
[ 16] Op Code: 5 (ADD ) R1:   10 R2:   12
[ 17] Op Code: 4 (STOR) R1:   10 R2:   12
[ 20] Op Code: 3 (LOAD) R1:   12 R2:   12
[ 23] Op Code: 3 (LOAD) R1:   12 R2:   13
[ 26] Op Code: 6 (SUB ) R1:   12 R2:    1
P8B Emulator: done executing at byte 27
```

As mentioned above, the program is supposed to evaluate this expression:

```
(4 + 9) - (10 + 2)
```

The first expression, 4 + 9, is evaluated at PC=6, leaving the result in register 2: R2=13. PC=7 stores the result in RAM for use later.

The second expression, 10 + 2, is evaluated at PC=16, leaving the result in register 2: R2=12. PC=17 stores the result in RAM for use later.

The two intermediate results are subtracted at PC=26 with the final result in register 2: R2=1.

So there you have it: a simple machine code program that does a simple job.

FASM 2.0: Variables

FASM 1.0 is fine as a proof-of-concept project, but the lack of variables is a drag. And the lack of output makes the whole exercise feel a bit pointless; I mean, the answer is there in R2 but that is unsatisfying somehow. To fix these issues, I added two new instructions to our virtual CPU and one macro assembler feature.

The two new instructions are very closely related: OUTN prints out "OUTPUT> " followed by the value of register 2 to the screen as a number. OUTS prints out "OUTPUT> " followed by the value of register 2 to the screen as a character.

The macro assembler feature is the DECL keyword which declares a variable by capturing a variable definition. This is an assembler feature because it generates no direct machine code output. Instead the DECL keyword makes the assembler remember the name and substitute the appropriate machine code for the name in the output. (This is the close cousin of the "compiler directive" which changes the compiler's behavior but does not generate any code directly.)

```
Op        Mne-
Code      monic    Description
----      -----    -----------
0         NOP      No operation
1         SET      Set a register's value
2         GET      Get a register's value
3         LOAD     Load a value from RAM
4         STOR     Store a value into RAM
```

```
5        ADD      Add R1 to R2
6        SUB      Subtract R1 from R2
7        OUTN     Output R2 as a number
8        OUTS     Output R2 as an alphanumeric
9        DECL     Declare a variable (not an instruction)
```

With the addition of these new features one can rewrite prog1 as prog2, new and improved. That program listing is in Appendix B.

Prog2 Variables

The second version of the assembler source, prog2.asm, is a tiny bit more legible with the ability to declare variables. Which brings up the question of what a variable actually is. I will take a brief look at this question here, but will return to it much greater detail down the road.

In our example, there are two variables: exp1, offset 0, length 1, data type byte and exp2, offset 1, length 1, data type byte. These are not very interesting declarations but they do illustrate how variables work.

So why do we care about variables and how they work? Because there are many cases in which bugs are caused by misuse of variables, by lack of understanding how they work and by confusion about what happens when one encounters more complex related concepts, such as structures and structure members. Trust me, some day you will be happy you know how variables are implemented.

OUTPUT OF PROG2

When you run prog2, you get this output:

```
P8B (Puny 8 Bit Processor) app
P8B Emulator  in: prog2.p8b 32 bytes
[  0] Op Code: 1 (SET ) R1:    4 R2:    0
[  3] Op Code: 1 (SET ) R1:    4 R2:    9
[  6] Op Code: 5 (ADD ) R1:    4 R2:   13
```

```
[  7] Op Code: 4 (STOR) R1:    4 R2:   13
[ 10] Op Code: 1 (SET ) R1:   10 R2:   13
[ 13] Op Code: 1 (SET ) R1:   10 R2:    2
[ 16] Op Code: 5 (ADD ) R1:   10 R2:   12
[ 17] Op Code: 4 (STOR) R1:   10 R2:   12
[ 20] Op Code: 3 (LOAD) R1:   12 R2:   12
[ 23] Op Code: 3 (LOAD) R1:   12 R2:   13
[ 26] Op Code: 6 (SUB ) R1:   12 R2:    1
[ 27] Op Code: 7 (OUTN) R1:   12 R2:    1
OUTPUT> 1
[ 28] Op Code: 1 (SET ) R1:   12 R2:   65
[ 31] Op Code: 8 (OUTS) R1:   12 R2:   65
OUTPUT> A
P8B Emulator: done at byte 32
```

A Note On Booting

Now I can talk about why I did not bring the Operating System into this discussion: there was no need. You do not need an O/S to run a program, although it sure helps. You can toggle a simple machine code program directly into a CPU's RAM and then metaphorically hit "go." That program will run--without the benefit of any O/S services or libraries, but it will run.

That simple machine code program has to load bytes from a memory location; if that memory location is the I/O buffer of a storage device, then bytes will be read off that storage device and into the CPU's memory.

This is how you start an O/S because an O/S is just another program and it is loaded and run just like any other program. Once the O/S is up and running, it runs other programs "under" it, and controls those other program's interactions with the CPU and with RAM and with the disk, but there is nothing magical about the O/S in the machine code context.

If the data read off that storage device is an O/S boot program, then your little machine code program is a "boot loader" and the location is the location of "Boot Sector" or "Master Boot Record" or "Boot program" or whatever that particular environment calls its boot software.

Starting an O/S is called "booting" because it is short for "boot strapping" which is a reference to the saying that disadvantaged people who succeed in life have "pulled themselves up by their boot straps" which is literally impossible and figuratively very hard. In the bad old days, using machine code to load a boot program (which usually loads a more complex boot program on top of itself, but that is another story) was that painful. Now that computers seem to "boot themselves" the analogy makes no sense but we are stuck with the jargon.

MORE ON BOOTING ☺

Very few people want to think about how their computer boots, let alone control the booting at every boot time, so instead of requiring human interaction, most booting occurs with some simplifying assumptions:

- Some piece of hardware is designated as the boot device, i.e. the place from which the boot loader will be loaded. This means that the boot loader does not have to ask from which device the boot program is to be loaded.

- The boot loader is kept in a default place, usually byte 0, which is the logical beginning of the boot device. This means that the boot loader does not have to ask where on the boot device to find the boot program.

- The boot program is no more than some default number of bytes long, usually 1024 bytes or some other power of 2. This means that the boot loader does not have to ask how many bytes to read from wherever it gets the boot program.

- There is often a built-in machine code (or even micro code) program in an Erasable Programmable Read-Only Memory chip (EPROM) which is what is run by the computer automatically at power-up and it checks the possible boot devices in some kind of order to a boot loader; in the usual Wintel PC, this program's configuration is managed by the BIOS. So the modern computer can, at power up, know which machine code to load and execute without human intervention.

SA: BOOTING IS INSECURE

Obviously there are many ways in which these assumptions can get you into trouble and the booting process is generally considered impossible to secure, hence the security truism that if someone can their hands on a computer, that computer should be considered compromised unless its data is encrypted.

Part of the booting security program comes from the fact that there is no O/S at boot time, so there is no software enforcing security policies.

Part of the booting security program comes from the fact that there is no difference between breaking into a working computer and re-covering a a broken one. In either case you direct the built-in pro-gram to a boot device of your choosing with a boot program of your choosing and do whatever you want with the computer once it is up and running your software. Since repairing computers is a well-documented and common activity, you will find vast amounts of advice on just how to do this on the Internet, which advice often assumes that you are not a thief and that you are not breaking into the computer. But there is no way to know what your intentions are. Just another case of context making all the difference.

FASM 3.0: The If-Statement

Before I talk about programming languages, I need to take a de-tour to get some appreciation of the humble if-statement because they are taken for granted and they are actually a pain to imple-ment.

(From a structural standpoint, it would be better to first encounter if-statements in the chapter on Logic but either I backtrack to op codes from Logic or I detour to if-statements in op codes before Logic. I am stubborn enough to want be done with op codes in this chapter, so here we are: a preview of if-statements so I can explain how they look from an op code perspective.)

I will assume that you are familiar with the if-statement but in the interests of clarity I will give the definition of if-statement that I are using. An if-statement has three possible clauses: the required if-clause, an optional else-if-clause and an optional else-clause.

The if-clause and the else-if-clause have the same form: an expression to be evaluated and an implicit branch. The else-clause has no expression and it is call an "unconditional branch."

If the expression evaluates to zero, it is considered 'false' and the associated block of code is executed (branched around). If the expression evaluates to one, it is considered 'true' and the associated block of code is executed. What if the expression is some other value? That case is usually not explicitly defined in theory; in practice almost every programming environment I have used treats all values except zero as "true" and zero is "false." I will return to this topic in detail in the logic chapter.

Let us consider the following if-statement, written in an imaginary programming language introduced below. This language should be easily comprehended, but for the record it is an ALGOL-style, line-based, block-oriented language. (It will become clear what all that means in the chapter on programming languages.)

```
if 5 equal 4 then
    output 'Y'
else
    output 'N'
endif
output 1
```

Since five is not equal to four, the code would output an N and then end with a 1. Just to confirm, I changed the code to compare four to four and it did output a Y and then end with a 1.

Alas, currently there is no support for this language, so what if I wanted the FASM assembler to do this?

In order to implement the equivalent of an if-statement, especially an if-statement that supports an else-clause, the CPU instruction set has to have two things added to it: an instruction to jump around, to implement even rudimentary control-flow and instructions to test values so that logical tests can be supported.

Specifically, I would need to add JMP which takes one argument, the PC to which to jump (remember, this will be zero-based). And I need to add BRNE which takes one argument, the PC to which to jump ("branch not equal") if R1 is not equal to R2.

Our Third FASM program, prog3.asm

So the new syntax is this:

```
Op        Mne-
Code      monic   Description
----      -----   -----------
0         NOP     No operation
1         SET     Set a register's value
2         GET     Get a register's value
3         LOAD    Load a value from RAM
4         STOR    Store a value into RAM
5         ADD     Add R1 to R2
6         SUB     Subtract R1 from R2
7         OUTN    Output R2 as a number
8         OUTS    Output R2 as an alphanumeric
9         DECL    Declare a variable (not an instruction)
10        BRNE    Branch if R1 not equal R2
11        JMP     Jump to a particular PC
```

Check out Appendix C for a listing of prog3.asm. Observe the branching and jumping. It takes a bit of bookkeeping to make sure that you are jumping to the right place. Man, is it great to have a compiler or interpreter do all that for you.

Here is what the output is, just as I expected:

```
P8B (Puny 8 Bit Processor) app
P8B Emulator  in: prog3.p8b 22 bytes
[  0] Op Code:  1 (SET ) R1:   4 R2:   0
[  3] Op Code:  1 (SET ) R1:   4 R2:   5
[  6] Op Code: 10 (BRNE) R1:   4 R2:   5
[  8] Op Code:  1 (SET ) R1:   4 R2:  78
[ 11] Op Code:  8 (OUTS) R1:   4 R2:  78
OUTPUT> N
[ 12] Op Code: 11 (JMP ) R1:   4 R2:  78
[ 18] Op Code:  1 (SET ) R1:   4 R2:   1
[ 21] Op Code:  7 (OUTN) R1:   4 R2:   1
OUTPUT> 1
```

```
P8B Emulator: done at byte 22
```

Self-Modifying Code (Assembler)

Instructions are just data in a buffer which are executed by the CPU. From that perspective, the instructions are just data in particular memory block. That means that an assembler program can modify itself by writing values into its memory block.

Why would anyone want to do that? A common use is configuration; for example, a colleague wrote an assembler program which handled the difference between two versions of the same CPU by modifying itself. Specifically, one version of the CPU had a feature that the other version did not. So the assembler code modified itself to jump around the code using that feature.

This way the program can adapt itself at run-time after detecting which CPU it is currently running on.

SA: Patching Binaries

There is a version of self-modifying code that happens before run-time: patching binaries.

Patching is the practice of making a small modification to software in order to solve a particular problem or problems.

Binaries are what we used to call executable images such as assembled programs. We had tools to set specified bytes of an executable to specified values. We used disassemblers to figure out which bytes at which offsets.

Patching binaries meant changing a compiler or assembled program without using an assembler or compiler, usually because we no longer had the sources or the development environment.

The last time I patched a binary, I had an old app which no longer worked because a long-standing premise was no longer valid. I could not recreate the app because the sources were no longer available. The options were to tell people whose jobs were easier with the app that they were out of luck, or to fire up a binary patch edit and set those bytes to their new values.

So why is this section a security alert? Because patching binaries is common way to get around security measures if you have a write-able copy of the binary executable. For instance, if you have a game for which you do not have a usage code. If you found the if-statement that tests to see if the user entered a valid code and over-write that code with a jump around the test so then you could run the binary executable without a valid code.

So my patching the binary was a legitimate work thing where I modified an executable that I owed. But a theoretical hacker patching a game to run it without paying for it. Same activity, different security implications. In security and in law, intent matters.

But how do you protect a binary against an attack when the binary is also a file on someone else's system and that someone is a privileged usc? It would help if you could make sure that there was no disassembler for your code but that would not guarantee anything because a machine code expect can nearly always do whatever they want. Luckily, every day more apps move to a client / server model and fewer and fewer machine code experts are made.

The Z80

For us, the P8B is a useful abstraction and teaching tool but there were 8 bit processors and they did useful work. Of these the most important was the Zilog Z80.

Armed with what you have learned from the P8B, you might find that there is much you can learn from the Z80.

Delve Deeper, Chapter 3

1. Look up the Zilog Z80 processor to see what a puny pro-cessor can do.

2. Find a copy of the Z80 instruction set and compare that in-struction set to P8B's instruction set.

3. Write a Z80 assembler program to substract 10 from 4.

4. Find a Z80 emulator and run your Z80 assembler program.

5. Run a disassembler on your Z80 programmer

6. Investigate ASCII; why was Unicode invented? What was ASCII missing?

Logic

This chapter is about two different things which are both called "logic." Specifically, I will be introducing predicate logic and bitwise operators and binary logic. It is rather hard to separate logic and bitwise operators from program execution control-flow (control-flow for short).

Why Is Logic Important To Programmers?

People tend to either enjoy formal logic or to find it rather boring. I see very little in between. Alas, most of the first group become logicians or mathematicians or philosophers. We can deduce, using logic, that most programmers are, alas, in the second group. Since I assume that you are a programmer, I have to assume that you may not really see the point to of all this. So this is my big chance to convince you. Which suddenly seems like a rather big hill to climb. But here goes:

PREDICATE LOGIC (CONTROL-FLOW)

We will cover control-flow in more detail below, but for now, here is the sales pitch:

• Software generally has three parts: input / process / output

• Process is has two parts: control-flow (logic) and operations

• Operations are often quite straightforward; control-flow is often mind-bendingly complex in aggregate

In other words, programmers cannot avoid control-flow and control-flow is critical. So studying it is a worthwhile exercise which will pay dividends.

BINARY LOGIC

There is no cleaner, simpler way to express binary conditions than binary logic. There is often no alternative to bit operations when dealing directly with hardware. So if you ever plan to write device drivers, or to debug hardware interactions, or to understand hardware interactions, you will need to brush up on your binary logic.

What Is Meant by "Logic" In This Context?

For our purposes in this simple overview, logic allows us to use rules to evaluate statements as being either "true" or "false" or "invalid." Each statement must either be true or false every time it is evaluated and each time that statement is evaluated the outcome must be the same. True statements are always true. False statements are always false.

Propositional logic evaluates propositions. For example, "all apples are fruits."

Premises are statements which are as-yet untested propositions which underly other statements. Premises are all-too-often unspoken or unconscious. This will be a big deal when we talk about debugging.

Predicate logic evaluates statements which have variables in them. For example, "my breakfast contains a piece of fruit." How do we know? We would have to enumerate the list of things I ate for breakfast and then plug each one into the predicate, making the predicate into a proposition which we can then evaluate.

```
thing (x) is a piece of fruit
```

where (x) is the "predicate variable" and in this case, a placeholder for each of the things in my breakfast.

It is tradition to introduce predicate logic by first going over propositional logic. So I will do that too, so that all the later texts you encounter will seem familiar.

Propositional logic consists of propositions which can be tested for being either true or false. We note that true can be represented by a one and false can be represented by zero. Hmmm.

In the context of logic, we call propositions which are true 'facts' and propositions which are not true 'false.' There are no shades of grey and no place for opinion or the right to your truth or reality. This is sometimes sad, but mostly refreshing.

Propositions are statements which can either be true or false. Examples are rather easy to come by: in fact, prog3.asm encoded a proposition and tested it. That proposition was this:

```
4 equals 5
```

And the result was false, which we represented as 'N' for "No."

However, most statements are not propositions. Let us quickly consider common statements types which are not propositions.

- Any statements which are subjective cannot be evaluated objectively. These are frequently matters of opinion. For example, "Batman movies all suck." Or "Chocolate is the best flavor of ice cream." Or "MacIntosh apples are the only good eating apples."

- Any statements which are about the unknowable cannot be evaluated, such as "My dog always knows exactly what I am thinking."

- Any statement which is self-contradictory cannot be evaluated, for example "This statement is false." So if the statement is true, then it is false, but if it false then it is true. This is part of kind of statement called in formal logic "a paradox."

- In fact, self-reference is a minefield for propositional logic. Consider this statement: "This statement is awesome in its unawesomeness."

- Any statement that is malformed or nonsensical cannot be evaluated, such as "Avocadoes thunder dance." In order to be able to evaluate a statement, that statement must first be comprehensible.

Limitations

The reason we are taking the time to think about logic in general and predicate logic in particular is the understand not its power but its limitations. Those who do not understand logic's limitations are bound to fall prey to those limitations.

Consistent, Not Correct

In the classic logic methodology, we start with premises, we proceed from those premises in a logical fashion and end up at logical conclusion. The rules guide us and, if properly applied, let us arrive at the logical endpoint.

The first thing to know about predicate logic is that philosophers tell us that any conclusion follows from a false premise. In other words logic allows us to arrive at a conclusion which is consistent with our rules and our premises.

For example, I assert that middle-aged men with grey beards are awesome. I observe that I am a middle-aged man with a grey beard. I conclude, therefore, that I am awesome.

Note that the flawed premise means that while there is no guarantee of correctness there is also no guarantee of failure. There is only uncertainty. In technology terms, there is a real chance that sometimes your flawed logic will work and sometimes it will fail.

Sadly, we must conclude that I may be either awesome or I may not.

Let us return to that very important difference between between consistency and correctness with an example. Let us imagine a perfect clock. Now imagine that this perfect clock is set to the wrong time. With its bad seed time, that clock will never be right. That perfect clock will work perfectly and its results will always be incorrect. That perfect clock's operations will be consistent with its premises and will follow the rules perfectly. The output will still be incorrect.

If the field of predicate logic guarantees only consistency with premises and not objective correctness, then we have the problem that if the premises are wrong, or the rules are misapplied, then the conclusion is invalid. For some reason, programmers only obsess about the rule application and not the premises. When technology fails, we grovel over our code but rarely stop to consider the premises.

Programmers often pride themselves on having "orderly" or "logical" minds and on being "reasonable." Too many programmers think that being logical or guided by reason assures correctness. It does not.

Here is the painful bottom line: if your premises are wrong, then your code can be correct and work correctly and still fail. Remember this when we talk about debugging down the line.

Flang

Once upon a time, we gave algorithms in an abstract sort-of programming language so that the reader could implement the algorithm in whatever language the reader was working. That was before programming texts starting picking particular languages.

This book continues that proud tradition: the examples will all be given in a faux programming language we call Flang.

Flang is a line-oriented, block-structured programming language much like Algol, hence we use the term "Algol-style."

The problem with line-oriented syntaxes is that sometimes need to write a very long line. For legibility, you want to break up those long lines across physical lines. The usual solution to this problem is to define a line continuation character, which is a character that means "ignore the end of line character to put all these lines together into a single line." For Flang, I will define a line continuation character "_' just like Visual BASIC.

Time Out For Sex

Some of the programming examples use the word "sex" to describe an attribute of human beings as stored in a database. Much of the target audience for this book is prone to finding this is distracting, alas. If this is you, take a minute to get over it. I'll wait.

Really. Sort it out. Work through it. Meditate. Giggle. Roll your eyes. Close your eyes and think of England. [1]

Great. Now we can get on with it.

Control-Flow (Logic)

In CS, "logic" almost always refers to controlling control-flow, by which we mostly mean if-statements. And if-statements just about always look like this Flang if-statement:

```
if-clause
    if-block
else-if-clause
    else-if-block
else-clause
    else-block
endif
```

This seems very simple and through familiarity it has become banal. We all know how it works. We all are comfortable with it. But too few of us really think about how to translate logical propositions into if-statements.

Let us consider a problem that a colleague used to use to see how good programmers were at this task:

old men and young women

This is clever because it requires handling two different competing attributes for the if-statement. Give this a whirl.

SPOILER ALERT: several possible answers follow. If you want to try it out, do not read ahead until you come up with your solution.

Really. Try it yourself first. No peeking.

Did you try it yourself?

Here's a page break to make it easier to avoid simply reading on.

```
if sex = 'M' and age >= old
    old-man-block
else if sex = 'F' and age <= young
    young-woman-block
endif
```

There are a number of common mistakes, mostly in the handling of the fact that we divide the population into male and female and we divide the population into young and old but we cannot do both simultaneously.

Premises

Remember the rant about premises? Here is the payoff for that. Let us consider premises and predicates.

In programming we can make the abstract more concrete. We can make our premises concrete when we are writing software, like this:

```
premise(sex == 'M' or sex == 'F')
premise(age >= 0 and age <= 125)

if (sex = 'M' and age >= old) or _
(sex = 'F' and age <= young)
    selected-block
endif
```

What does the "premise()" function do? Well, that depends on the context: if the software is a User Interface, perhaps premise() function sends a message to the user. If the software is a service routine, then perhaps premise() should log the error for analysis later.

Predicates

Part of what is interesting about "old men and young women" problem is the vagueness of the concepts "old" and "young." Controlling vagueness is what programming predicates do best.

In programming we call functions which return either a one or a zero "boolean functions." Predicates are boolean functions we use to make our control-flow logic clearer or easier to maintain.

In Lisp, the convention is to end a Lisp predicate with a "P" for predicate, for example "evenp" which tests a numeric value for having the property of being evenly divisible by 2.

In C, the convention is to begin a C predicate with "is" such as the library function "isspace" which tests a character for the property of being whitespace (a blank, or a tab, or a newline or a carriage return).

In Flang, predicates are procedures whose names end with a question mark, like this: "predicate?".

USING PREDICATES

Now let us try that selection problem:

The predicates old? and young? are probably obvious, because these concepts are vague. It might not be clear why I defined male? or female? but that was force of habit: after years of working with medical data I know that the sex attribute is often one of these:

• Male

• Female

• Other

• Unknown

How do you count 'Other' and / or 'Unknown'? I don't know but using the predicates makes that decision clear when the reader finds the single, consistent definition of male or female. The predicate is a way of stating your premises.

```
if male?(sex) and old?(age)
    old-man-block
else if female?(sex) and young?(age)
    young-woman-block
endif
```

This assumes that we only want one bucket (see below). This is fine, assuming that the old-man-block and young-woman-block are the same code. That is a question I will return to below.

How about this as a solution?

```
if (male?(sex) and old?(age)) or _
(female?(sex) and young?(age))
    selected-block
endif
```

LOGIC BUCKETS

If-statements do a number of jobs, but often they are used to sort elements into separate groups, informally called "buckets" hence "logic buckets."

If-statements can handle a particular case of input, like this:

```
if (age > limit)
    set age to limit
endif
```

If-statements can divide the input into two buckets, usually accept / reject or select / reject:

```
if (valid?(input))
    Process_input(input)
```

```
else
    Report_error(input)
endif
```

If-statements can divide the input into several buckets:

```
if (newborn?(age))
    new-born-block
else if (baby?(age))
    baby-block
else if (child?(age))
    child-block
else if (adult?(age))
    adult-block
else if (elderly?(age))
    elderly-block
else
    Report_error(input)
endif
```

When we are write if-statements we should consider the number of buckets into which we want to put input.

In the original problem, "old men and young women," we should ask how many buckets we want to end up with because that will determine how the if-statement should be structured.

Economy Verus Efficiency

Some programmers confuse economy of expression with efficiency of execution.

Economy of expression in this context refers to writing code with the fewest number of characters [2] .

Efficiency of execution in this context refers to writing code that produces a program which runs as quickly as possible.

BENEFITS OF ECONOMY OF EXPRESSION

The shorter source code is, the easier it is to keep all in your head at once, which makes modifying it easier and safer. This assumes that the economic expression is intelligible. Making your code brief at the expense of making it readable is generally a terrible choice.

BENEFITS OF EFFICIENCY OF EXECUTION

The smaller a package of machine code is the faster it loads and often the faster it runs and lower its load on the underlying hardware. This assumes that the efficient runable image works correctly. Making your code efficient at the expense of making it correct is generally a terrible choice.

PROS AND CONS

Sometimes economically expressed code produces efficient machine code; often it does not. Sometimes efficiency is very important; sometimes it is not. This topic will come up again as part of considering these trade-offs in the chapter on computer languages.

For now, I consider the economy of expression in the specific domain of if-statements and through the lens of clarity, because the execution speed of if-statements is rarely a problem.

When you write if-statements, you are controlling execution flow in your code. You should be striving to make your control-flow accurate and clear to other programmers (which group includes your future self).

This is a long way of saying that you should generally resist the urge to make the clauses of your if-statements cryptic. Be as clear as you can.

One way to make your if-statements and control-flow clearer is to separate the decision making from the execution.

```
if PoorAttendance?() or (Homework?() < ok)_
or TestScores? < ok
    FailStudent()
endif


FailFlag = false
if PoorAttendance?()
    FailFlag = true
else if (Homework?() < ok)
    FailFlag = true
else if TestScores? < ok
    FailFlag = true
endif

if FailFlag
    FailStudent()
endif
```

Bitwise Operations

This may seem like a strange digression, but we are going to consider bitwise operations.

Operations are done by operators which operate on operands.

Bitwise operations operate on bits; the most common ones are "And", "Or" and "Not". Both And and Or are "dyadic" or "binary" which means that they take two operators: by convention, the two operators are often called "the lefthand side" (LHS) and "the righthand side" (RHS). The Not operator is "monadic" or "unary" which means that it takes only one operator: an RHS.

Bitwise operators return a result, which is called "the return value."

Bitwise And

Bitwise And runs through a LHS bitstring, comparing each LHS bit to its RHS counterpart; if the LHS bit is true and the RHS bit is true, the output bit is true; otherwise the output bit is false. The return value is the output bitstring. For example:

```
LHS 01100101
RHS 01010101
    --------
 RV 01000101
```

Bitwise Or

Bitwise Or runs through a LHS bitstring, comparing each LHS bit to its RHS counterpart; if the LHS bit is true or the RHS bit is true, the output bit is true; otherwise the output bit is false. The return value is the output bitstring.

```
LHS 01100101
RHS 01010101
    --------
 RV 01010101
```

Bitwise Not

Bitwise Not runs through a RHS bitstring and returns true for false and false for true. The return value is the output bitstring.

```
NOT 01010101
    --------
 RV 10101010
```

BITWISE OPERATIONS IN ACTION

This is the output of the very simple C program (source code in Appendix D) which demonstrates basic bitwise operations. In the C programming language, the bitwise And operator is "&" and the bitwise Or operator is "|" and the bitwise Not operator is "!":

```
Logical And
0 & 0...false
1 & 1...true
0 & 1...false

Logical Or
0 | 0...false
1 | 1...true
1 | 0...true

Testing values to see if they are true
-1 is...true
 0 is...false
 2 is...true
```

Bit Flags

Bitwise operators do not work on single bits but rather on all the bits in the numeric values that they are given. In a programming context, bitwise operators work on all the bits in a byte, or all the bits in any other longer numeric values.

When we consider each bit in a bitstring as a separate Boolean flag, those bits are called "bit flags."

BIT MASKS

We can set bit flags, or clear them or test them, all by means of a list of bits which we call "a bit mask." The bit mask is a number which only as the bits we want turned on, to make And-ing and Or-

ing possible. Alas, there is no programming environment of which
I am aware which supports actual bit strings as a numeric constant,
so we have to be somewhat creative in our bit specification:

Bit	Mask	Decimal	Octal	Hex
0	00000001	1	001	0x1
1	00000010	2	002	0x2
2	00000100	4	004	0x4
3	00001000	8	010	0x8
4	00010000	16	020	0x10
5	00100000	32	040	0x20
6	01000000	64	0100	0x40
7	10000000	128	0200	0x80

As an example, let us consider a function which looks up a person's name in a database. Further, let us say that this function can
encounter the following errors:

	Error	Bit Mask	Decimal
1	Database I/O error	00000001	1
2	Input name is blank	00000010	2
3	Input Name not found	00000100	4
4	Multiple name records matched	00001000	8

SET A BIT FLAG

You set a bit flag like this:

1. Construct the appropriate mask: a integer whose only "on" bit is the bit you want to set

2. Declare an integer variable to hold the flag or flags

3. Set that integer variable to the value returned by the bitwise Or of the bit flags variable with the mask.

```
int bit_flags;
bit_flags = (bit_flags | mask);
```

TEST A BIT FLAG

You test a bit flag like this:

1. Construct the appropriate mask: a integer whose only "on" bit is the bit you want to test

2. Declare an integer variable to hold the flag or flags

3. Get the result of the bitwise AND of the bit flag variable with the mask

4. If that result is a 1 then the bit flag is set or "true"; if the result is zero then the bit flag is unset or "false."

CLEAR A BIT FLAG

You clear a bit flag like this:

1. Construct the appropriate mask: a integer whose only "on" bit is the bit you want to test

2. Declare an integer variable to hold the flag or flags

3. Use the bitwise Not operator to create an inverse of the mask, in other words a integer value where each bit is the opposite of the mask, so the bit we want to clear is the only bit which is zero / off / false. Let us call this the "bit clearing mask."

4. Set the integer to the value of a bitwise And with the bit clearing mask.

Check out Appendix E for the some C source code which does some basic bit flag manipulation; here is that output:

```
Setting all the flags...
mask=1, bit_flags= 1 error=Database I/O
mask=2, bit_flags= 3 error=Blank Name
mask=4, bit_flags= 7 error=Name Not Found
mask=8, bit_flags=15 error=Multiple Names Matched

Testing all the flags...
mask=1, bit_flags=15 rv=1
mask=2, bit_flags=15 rv=2
mask=4, bit_flags=15 rv=4
mask=8, bit_flags=15 rv=8

Clearing all the flags...
mask=1, bit_flags=14
mask=2, bit_flags=12
mask=4, bit_flags=8
mask=8, bit_flags=0
```

MULTIPLE BIT FLAGS

Our examples consider only one bit flag at a time, but there is no reason that an integer value can't have more than one bit flag set or tested or cleared. Thus a single bit flags value can hold multiple flags.

Bit flags are also a reasonable way to represent attributes. We used to use bit flags to search records as a kind of index, but that is a story for another chapter.

UNIX RETURN CODES: AN HISTORICAL NOTE ☺

Unix programmers may have noticed a strange convention: Unix programs generally return zero for "all's well" and some other value for "there was a problem." So they return "false" for "all is well" and "true" for "there was a problem or problems."

This came about because it was simplest to return an integer from either a function or a program. On all of those early systems, an integer was 16 bits wide, or two bytes.

As an unsigned quantity, a two byte integer can hold 65,536 values, or 32,768 values as a signed value. That gave us a vast range of possible error codes, but what if we wanted to return multiple error conditions at once? Instead of a vast range of error codes, we often considered those bite as up to 16 bit flags.

This meant that we could use the following programming idioms in C:

```
if (function(arg1,arg2)) { /* check for any error */
        /* hand an error */
}

if ((rc = function(arg1,arg2))) { /* check for any error */
        /* hand an error */
        if ((rc & ERROR_MASK_1) == 1) {
                /* handle this error */
        }
        if ((rc & ERROR_MASK_2) == 1) {
                /* handle that error */
        }
        if ((rc & ERROR_MASK_3) == 1) {
                /* handle the other error */
        }
}
```

Control Flow Logic

So now we arrive at our destination for this chapter: control-flow logic, bitwise and otherwise.

We already slipped in the logical And and logical Or concepts in the if-statement section. Bitwise And and bitwise Or work very similarly. In fact, you can use them both together, especially if you have set the bit flags based on attributes:

```
if (bits & MALE) and (bits & OLD)
        Do_Old_Men()
else if (bits & FEMALE) and (bits & YOUNG)
        Do_Young_Women()
endif
```

In a way, we use Boole's algebra as he had hoped, to implement logical statements. You may never need to know how bits work, but now you know where to look if you ever end up needing to know.

Delve Deeper, Chapter 4

1. Want to know about logic in general and logic in computer science in specific? Go deeper into any of the many perfectly serviceable references on the web. Search for "predicate logic" and "predicate logic in computer science."

```
Look up the dreaded dangling else:
https://en.wikipedia.org/wiki/Dangling_else
```

1. look up Algol and try to appreciate its ethereal beauty and its pioneering, trail blazing place in computer science.

2. Do you need premise() and predicates?

3. What do some people want to specify bit masks in Octal or Hexadecimal?

Chapter 4 End Notes

[1] This is a hilarious historical reference: Google it.

[2] By character, we mean any member of a character set, basically anything you can type on a keyboard.

Programming Languages

This chapter is about programming languages in which software is written.

Natural Languages

Natural languages arise naturally, as part of a given culture and given historical era. Natural languages usually incorporate elements of languages which went before. Natural languages change and evolve in response to changing needs and norms. Natural languages do not have distinct authors but rather many authors making relatively small contributions over relatively long periods of time.

Natural languages are primarily expressive: they generally allow us to express thoughts and hopes and feelings as well as facts and observations.

Formal Languages

Formal languages are also human constructs, but in a more formal and more deliberate sense. Formal languages are usually intended to perform a specific function.

Computer Languages

Computer Programming languages are a subset of formal languages intended to allow people to write software or to control computer resources. These two completely different models of what computer languages are for will show again later in this chapter and in later chapters. I will call the first model "literary" and the second model "engineering" just because I will need names later and there are no existing, accepted terms for these competing models.

Human Artifact

Whenever I think about technology, or am introduced to a technology, or try to use a new technology, I fall back on an essential truth. Technology is a human artifact, made by people for people and the usual five W's apply:

1. Who (made the technology)

2. Why (did they make it)

3. When (did they make it)

4. Where (did they make it)

5. What (did they use to make it)

Programming Languages vs Programming

Just as it is hard to separate a natural languages from its cultural context so it is hard to separate a programming language from its context. Therefore I will talk a bit about programming even as I try to focus on the languages themselves.

Some programmers try to make their computer programs as short as possible, in the mistaken belief that a short chunk of programming language will generate a short chunk of machine code which will execute quickly.

Whenever we talk about human beings writing computer programs (coding), we talk about balancing these three criteria:

1. Effectiveness: software that does not do what it is supposed to do is a special case of 'broken.' Working is the ultimate goal.

2. Efficiency: software which consumes more resources than it can afford is wasteful and has trouble scaling up.

3. Elegance: software which is inelegant, which is hard to read and difficult to change, becomes an ever-increasing burden

to maintain.

The Autodidact's Blind Spots

Let us revisit the case for Computer Science even if you never want to be an academic. In a nutshell, the academic approach is designed to compensate for human failings, much like the scientific method. The academic approach is supposed to force us to be well-founded and rigorous in our approach to a given subject. It is supposed to help us avoid our blind spots and prejudices and unconscious biases.

When I first stepped onto a college campus as a student in Agust of 1980, I was already a programmer. I had first come in contact computers and programming in middle school, using paper tape to store and load my BASIC programs. The computer was special and distant: I used a teletype terminal with the paper tape to interact with the distant computer. That terminal was in a closet because terminals were rarely-used and somewhat noisy things. I wrote programs which allowed me to use the computer as a pretty powerful pocket calculator. Well, powerful in 1970's terms.

In high school I was there when the first desktop computer arrived, an MS-DOS machine with a much better interface and more powerful operating system and an even more powerful BASIC interpreter. I was just about the only person, student or faculty, who knew how to actually make it do useful work, so they let me program my physics labs' homework.

So by the time I was in college, I thought that I was an experienced expert: I knew how to use a computer as a simple calculator and I was highly confident that this was all a computer could do.

I was much more interested in formal languages that in computer hardware. I was much more into semantics and semiotics than into bits and bytes. I moved on from BASIC to C and then things started going a bit wrong: I was living in a 16 bit world without knowing what that meant.

Usually, living in a 16 bit world did not matter, but then I found that the result of adding one to 32,768 was -1. That was unexpected, because I was ignorant. I found that I could fix the problem with values over 32,768 by declaring my "int" to be "unsigned" so long as I did not want negative numbers and then I could get to 65,535 before I hit 0 again, sometimes with an "overflow error."

I quickly tired of running into brick walls I did not even know were there. I swallowed my pride and I gritted my teeth and humbled myself and starting taking CS courses.

I loved the formal linguistics. I was lukewarm to the electrical engineering. But I really benefited from being forced to cover topics I would not have chosen. Because autodidacts have blind spots and they do not even know those blind spots are there. Because the blind spots are self-reinforcing: it is very hard to know what you do not know, so it is very hard to fix your blind spots.

Imagine how small my world would be today as a former BASIC programmer turned FORTRAN programmer who specializes in scientific programming. Now imagine how you will look in 35 years if you stick with whatever programming language you are using now and with whatever bag of tricks you arc using now. Grow. Learn in an organized, efficient way. Avoid becoming a dinosaur which happens so quickly in our industry.

(You will likely never live in a 16 bit world; currently the world is 64 bit and may someday be 128 bit. But there are still issues you will blunder into unaware and there is still the faint chance that you will have to program for a device which is not a computer and not 64 bit. But you fall off the edge of whatever abstraction you are using and you will land with a thud on the harsh realities of physics and hardware. We all do, sooner or later. It is as inescapable as entropy.)

Vegetarian Food

I am not a fan of vegetables. I am far closer to being a carnivore than a herbivore. Somewhat ironically, my first living situation after college was with two housemates were vegetarians. In years of living together, I made some surprising discoveries:

- Frittatas are a quick and tasty meal, even veggie frittatas. They are easy to make. They work as an entry for brunch or lunch or dinner. They pair nicely with many white wines.

- Mushroom crepes are delicious. They really are, in all their meatless glory.

- Veggie kabobs make a terrific side-dish for a meat eater at a bar-beque.

- Vegetarian chocolate cheese cake is a delightful dessert.

Without someone else to force me to learn new things, I would never have tried these things. I was certain that I would not like them. I was wrong. I thought that writing short BASIC programs to do high school physics was as cool as computer programming could get. I was wrong. If you get comfortable with a few things, it is easy to get into a rut without realizing it.

An academic background can help round out your worldview. It can help you avoid being that guy / gal who thinks that the programming language you learned the best choice for all projects. It can help you avoid being that guy / gal who thinks that whatever data platform you first encountered is the only one. It can help you avoid being that guy / gal who does not even know what they don't know.

Effort versus Excellence

This topic is difficult to discuss because it is as much about psychology as it is about programming. Since so many of us get into programming to get away from human beings and the messy psychology that comes with us, discussing such things does not come easy or generally go well. Brace yourself: it is about to get a bit touchy-feely in here--but not for long, I promise.

Asymmetry

In order to properly consider Effort versus Excellence I need to introduce the Point of View (POV) concept. PoV exercises exist to prove a point: many human interactions are asymmetric. In practice. this means that many behaviors are fun to do to others but no fun to have them done to us. This seems like kindergarten wisdom, but it is true none the less: fun to dish out, no fun to deal with. We all have this problem but we differ wildly in our awareness of it and our ability to compensate for it.

The two points of view in this discussion are the programmer and the teammate. Most of us end up in jobs or situations where we are sometimes the programmer and sometimes the teammate and transit from one to the other many times a day.

The Perils of Effort

The programmer often falls prey to rather unfortunate human trait: we fall in love with our pain. If something was hard for us to do, we tend to value that thing beyond its actual value. Just because it was hard to do does not mean it is good, but it does mean that the programmer tends to get attached.

This attachment is hard for the teammate because this attachment makes it harder for the teammate to give feedback. I was one of the teammates to a programmer who spent three days struggling to create a function that is readily available in a library. And the programmer's version, not surprising, was not as good as the library function which had more programmer hours and more feedback and more eyes on it. It was painful to have to say "My God, why did you waste all that time?" instead of the expected response which I gather was "My God, you're a genius! You did all that in only three days!"

I am sure that various of my teammates have very, very similar stories about me as a programmer. We all do it, but that does not mean that we should accept it; it means that we should strive to do it less.

The Joys of Being Effective

Another reason that this trait is particularly unfortunate for the autodidact is that as we teach ourselves new tricks, we tend to avoid learning the existing ways of doing those tricks.

In most cases, learning the existing ways is faster, more efficient and more effective than re-inventing the wheel. Not always, but usually. Don't worry, the tendency of programmers to re-invent the wheel is strong: resisting it does not mean that it will never happen. It will happen plenty of times. But if you stop to consider how teammates will see your work, your work will be better and your work life will be better.

Running Program (Languages)

Let us return to our usual starting point, a running program.

In this context, programming languages, a running program is the result of either compiling the source code into machine code or interpreting the source code as machine code. In either case, we start with source code and end up with a package of instructions for the CPU which has been loaded into RAM to become a running process.

In this context I will not ignore the role of the Operating System in turning that package of instructions into a process, but I will not focus on it either until the chapter on Operating Systems.

Two New Concepts

As part of covering the running program, I will be using the terms "platform" and "environment" and so I will define them here.

THE PLATFORM

A running program runs on a piece of hardware, usually under an Operating System. The combination of the hardware and system software is usually called "the platform."

THE ENVIRONMENT

The combination of the platform and supporting libraries and other supporting software is what I refer to as "the environment."

THE DIFFERENCE

These are very related concepts and I want to make sure that they do not blur together in your mind. Here are some platform versus environment pairs:

1. The Java Virtual Machine is an environment; Windows and Linux are both platforms on which the JVM runs.

2. The Perl interpreter and its modules form an environment; Windows and Linux are both platforms on which Perl runs.

3. I would argue that iOS, with its extensions is an environment and the iPhone and iPad are platforms.

The Running Program

On the journey from source code to running machine code, I start with a single statement. (Note that many programming languages are not line-based so sometimes a statement spans lines.)

Grammar

Some people use "grammar" and "syntax" interchangeably; I find this practice very confusing.

Like their natural language counter-parts, formal languages have a grammar. When I use the term, I mean the strict definition which is roughly "the completely collection of rules and conventions governing the construction of legal statements in that language."

Grammar's rules operate on lexemes; a lexeme is roughly what a natural language speaker would call "a word" except that there are some lexemes which are not quite words, such as "+" or "/" which are not punctuation and not what a speaker would call a "word."

In these terms, syntax is a part of a grammar. So what does syntax mean?

Syntax

Syntax is the set rules for what to do with lexemes: what order they can be in, which lexemes go with which other lexemes, etc.

Computer Languages

While there are many different programming languages, there are only a few different ways to programming language statements into machine code:

COMPILED

With a compiled programming language, a compiler takes in large blocks of computer code and produces a large block of machine code; these large blocks are compiled objects; these objects are then linked into executable programs. FORTRAN and ALGOL are the ancient gods of compiled languages. The C programming language is one of the few left standing.

INTERPRETED

With an interpreted programming language, an interpreter takes in a statement or statement-block and then creates machine code which is then executed within the interpreter or "run-time environment." The original BASIC is an example of a purely interpreted language, as is Ruby.

PSUEDO-COMPILED, PSUEDO-INTERPRETED

With a psuedo-compiled, psuedo-interpreted a compiler compiles source not into machine code, but into psuedo-code which is a simplified or specialized version of machine code, designed to be input to the psuedo-interpreter. The original hybrid programming language, so far as I know, is Pascal. The most widely used is probably Java. Perl and Python are both examples of this kind of programming language.

RIPPLE EFFECTS

The translation category in which the programming language falls has an effect on its syntax and its look-and-feel ("what it is like to use it").

The Usual Process

In the general case, statements in computer languages go through these steps:

1. Lexing: turning a source statement into lexemes. There are more or less generic tools which can handle this job.

2. Parsing: making sure that the collection of lexemes conforms to the syntax and building a machine-readable version of the statement. There are fewer generic tools for doing this job, since it requires the ability to represent the syntax in such a way that a parser can tell whether or not the statement is legal.

3. Machine Code Generating: running through the parse tree and creating machine code for the target computer. This is a rather specialized programming task, requiring a deep understanding of the target environment's machine code.

Cross-Compiling

In the usual case, the machine code generation is done in the environment in which the code will run. But generating code for the "native" environment is not the only case: there is nothing to stop a compiler from generating machine code for another environment (or "platform"). When machine code is generated for a target other than the native platform, that is called "cross-compiling" because you compile in one environment and run in another.

A common case for cross-compiling is the development of software for a limit or novel platform, such as a system to be "embedded" in an appliance. Cross-compiling spares the appliance developer the task of creating a development environment in addition to the appliance's intended purpose. Furthermore, the target may lack the computing power to generate machine code either effectively or quickly.

Cross-compiling is also how many new environments get their first version of software needed to build software for that new environment. In order to have a compiler for a given platform, the first version has to be created somewhere, almost never on the new platform itself.

Linking

For compiled languages there are logical units, blocks of code which are compiled and then written out as object files. These object files are not runable: before they can be loaded and run as programs they have to be "linked" together.

The compiler leaves some questions unanswered and these questions have to be resolved by the linker before the linked together program can run as a program. For instance, every variable has to be declared, but only once. The linker goes through all the objects making sure that references to the variable all refer to the same memory location and that each variable is declared at least once but no more than once.

Even if you write a completely self-contained application, that application will almost certainly require services from the operating system and quite likely functions from libraries. Libraries are little databases of compiled objects, structured to make the linker's life easier when searching for library functions and resolving calls to library functions.

Deciding where to put functionality--in the compiler, in application libraries, in system libraries or in the O/S itself--is a major decision point.

(Remember this for when we talk about debugging. Sometimes the O/S exposes parts of itself through Application Program Interfaces (API) which are in libraries; sometimes the functionality is in the libraries themselves. This is a distinction which rarely matters, but when it does matter, it matters very much.)

Choosing A Language

The most common reason I hear for choosing the programming language boils down to "I chose the one I know." I suppose that this is a good enough reason if a given programmer only knows one programming language, but I would expect a good programmer to be able to transfer his or her skills from one environment to another. I would expect a good programmer to be curious about various development environments and to explore them to be ready for tasks as they arise.

For any given programming task, there are many factors to consider when choosing the development environment, assuming that you have a choice. (Some target devices have only one credible development environment; some run-time environments offer few options from which to choose.)

How do programming languages stack up against each other? This is the sort of question which starts long and bitter arguments and if you are not careful, these arguments are about personal preference masquerading as science.

PERSONAL PREFERENCES

The first questions you have to ask yourself are about yourself, so that you have some faint chance of making your prejudices and preferences a reasonable and known part of the equation.

Personally, I am not a big fan of typing. I like my programming languages to be terse. This is a real bias of mine; for example, I really dislike programming in Visual BASIC with the endless typing, the long, case-sensitive names with their endless dot-notation names. Is this a good reason for me to avoid Visual BASIC? In many situations, I found no credible alternative, so I use it.

Personally, I mostly enjoy team programming, but I dislike being part of a large team. What does this about team programming versus large teams? Not much.

Personally, I like using the Unix operating system and its derivatives so I end up doing quite a bit of programming in Perl and C and the Bourne Shell. Do I feel that these are the best programming languages? Depends.

Personally, I like learning new programming languages and it comes easily enough to me that I find learning a new programming language for even a single project is not a burden. I end up writing code that looks very much like the examples from which I am working. Is that a good thing or a bad thing? I am not sure.

These are statements about me. They are important to me and quite possibly the people for whom I work and with whom I work. But they are not science. They are true, but only about my subjective experience.

Think about your preferences and prejudices. Take an inventory of yourself. Be honest. Having preferences and prejudices is fine. Pretending that you don't is not fine. Pretending paints you into uncomfortable corners, it makes you worse as a programmer and a bad teammate. Be better as a programmer. Be a better teammate.

THE FIVE W'S AGAIN

When choosing a programming language, it is often helpful to use the five W's as a framework:

1.   Who is the audience for the software? User Experience (UX) often narrows the list of which development environments you can use.

2.   Why is the software being made? The overall goal usually dictates how long you have, how many people you can use and all these factors also narrow the list.

3.   When is a tricky question. If your software is only going to be used for a relatively short period of time, you can use a mature, familiar environment. If you have a long planning horizon, using a mature, familiar environment risks having your development environment being outdated or obsolete.

4.   Where is the software going to run? Deployment is a huge part of the effort of support software, if you are going to distribute the software to many instances or many different kinds of instance or both.

5.   What is the software supposed to do? There is huge overlap between the functionality of development environments and run-time environments, but the overlap is far from perfect. There are many features only available in some environments. Sometimes key functionality you need is "built-in" to some environments and not others.

Let us take a detour to what is built-in and what is not.

COMPILER DIRECTIVES

In compiled languages, there are special statements which do not contribute directly to the machine code being generated but instead help the compiler do its job. Sometimes compiler directives are handled by a completely separate program, such as the C pre-processor. Compiler directives sometimes confer a big advantage to compiled languages over interpreted languages, because compiler directives can provide a real measure of control over how software is put together.

PRIMITIVES

Some data types are built-in for use by any software written in a given programming language. Other data types are defined by the programmer for the program. The usual primitive data types include "integer" and "character" and "floating point number."

How fussy a programming language is about data types used to be called "strongly typed" for the very fussy and "weakly typed" for the not very fussy. The fussiness is either a compiler's ability to make sure that your treatment of a particular variable is consistent, or the interpreter's ability to complain about what values you try to assign to a particular variable.

In order to understand how to use a programming language, you need to know what is offered in the way of primitives and to know how easy a given programming language makes it for you to define and fill and access your own complex data types and structures.

INTRINSICS

Some functions are built-in for use by any software written in a given programming language. These functions are part of the programming language specification or standard installation. Sometimes the functionality is provided by libraries which are considered part of the compiler environment. Sometimes the compiler actually generates machine code directly into the compiled object files. This is not a distinction which matters much, until it does. This is yet another topic which will be covered under the "debugging" rubric.

Dynamic Linking

The process of taking a bunch of compiled objects and creating a runable image is called "static linking." This was the original way in which all linking worked, so people usually just say "linking."

But then dynamic linking was invented, so programmers needed a new term, to help us to distinguish the new kind of library, the Dynamic Link Library (DLL).

Dynamic linking is just what is sounds like: some of the questions which are resolved by static linking are left unresolved by dynamic linking, which forces the run-time environment to resolve them. This breaks the simple "load-and-execute" paradigm but it provides some very attractive advantages as well as some serious drawbacks.

```
+--------------------+----------------------+
| Pros               | Cons                 |
+--------------------+----------------------+
| Configurability    | Fragility            |
+--------------------+----------------------+
| Updates & Upgrades | Run-time performance |
+--------------------+----------------------+
| Search Path        | Search Path          |
+--------------------+----------------------+
| Cross Environments | Difficult to Debug   |
+--------------------+----------------------+
```

PROS

- Configurability means the ability to customize a system for particular platforms while keeping the core of the software the same. It is not an accident that DLLs were embraced by Microsoft who controlled not only the O/S but the apps as well. They could put functionality in their O/S for all of their apps to share because they knew that the "system DLLs" would always there because Microsoft could ensure that.

- Updates & Upgrades means changing delivered software without having to do a major release. In evolutionary biology, there is the concept of "point evolution": the grass evolves so the cow evolves to compensate. There is no forward progress, but rather maintaining of the *status quo*. There is a depressing amount of similar activity in the software game: the O/S functions change slightly so the apps have to change to match. This kind of update or upgrade is ideally handled by good design which puts the likely-to-change code in a DLL which can be sent out whenever the O/S or application framework changes. Even better, the O/S vendor can take care of it for you.

- Search Path means the directories and files the run-time environment searches for DLLs for unresolved function calls, and the order in which to search them. A properly constructed search path reduces the chance that the wrong version will be found in the wrong DLL.

- Cross Environments means that you can mix and match from different development languages in a single application. For instance, I often provide specialized functionality written in C but run by Visual BASIC apps or MS-Office apps.

CONS

- Fragility means that the reliance on DLLs causes that piece of software to be fragile: in order to work correctly, an app which calls DLLs relies on the DLLs being present and correct. Since DLLs are often shared across apps, there is the very real possibility that another app will overwrite a DLL you need with a newer, "better" version which causes your app to suddenly start to fail. Even though your app is mature and unchanged.

- Run-Time Performance means the time and resources required for the run-time environment to execute the search for the right DLL, then load the right code out of the right DLL and then resolve the open questions and then set up a jump of the PC from the main app to the loaded DLL function (and back, if need be).

- Search Path means the directories and files the run-time environment searches for DLLs for unresolved function calls, and the order in which to search them. A badly constructed search path increases the chance that the wrong version will be found in the wrong DLL.

• Difficult to Debug means that debugging the interaction between the app and DLL, let alone the DLL itself, especially since one often does not have the source code for the DLL.

Development Environments

In this chapter, I will often use "programming language" as a shorthand for the combination of the computer programming language's grammar, the compiler and/or interpreter and the various libraries or gems or DLLs or system calls or other supporting software and perhaps even an Integrated Development Environment (IDE) such as Microsoft Studio. Sometimes a development environment is tied to a particular O/S and is hard to separate from that O/S. (Machine code is the ultimate in O/S-bound development.)

I will try to use "programming language" when I mean the semantics and grammar of a particular programming language, but when talking about using a programming language, it is hard to avoid talking about the development environment.

All of the attributes of a development environment can make a given programming job faster or slower to complete, easier or harder to complete, easy to maintain or difficult to maintain.

Design Paradigm Review

A classic is something that everybody wants to have read and nobody wants to read.

 Mark Twain

With apologies to Twain, design paradigms are something that every programmer wants to have studied but nobody wants to study.

I think that many programmers learn at least one design paradigm, but it is often only one and often the one required by whatever very high-level programming language they first learn. I think that too many programmers never study the topic of design paradigms. The following section is my attempt to get us all on the same design paradigm page.

In other words, I feel that I cannot count on my audience have a uniform or shared familiarity with design paradigms. I feel forced to cover this territory even though many of you will be bored or turned off. Skim or skip with my blessing but come back here if you find that later parts are not making sense.

Design Paradigms ☺

Software is just like any other kind of authoring or building project: you need a blueprint. You can write an essay without an outline or a rough draft, without an idea of what you want to say or to whom you want to say it, but this is not recommended. And "going for it" really only works if there is only one of you.

For most applications, for most teams and for most projects, the first step is a design.

In the Machine Code Age and in the early "High Level Language" age (where "high level" meant "higher than machine code"), access to the computer was the most expensive resource. We did not have easy access to the computer; in fact, our time was measured in minutes and "machine time" was precious. We were pretty sick of the oft-repeated carpenter's motto, "think twice, cut once." To us, this meant "slave over the code before you try to compile it" and "do as much debugging in your head before your precious turn at the CPU."

In this model, the scope of what we could achieve was limited. The process was mapped out like this:

• Requirements: what is the software supposed to do?

• Specifications: what exactly is the software going to do?

• Implementation: coding the "specs" as closely as possible

• Unit testing: making sure that each software unit works properly

• User acceptance: having actual users try it out (UA)

• Debugging cycle: get feedback from UA, write up bug reports, fix the bugs, kick back to UA.

As computers became faster and more available, the entire process became compressed. Programmers could code more and test more and "stepwise refinement" came into vogue. We could code and test and code and test and try out possibilities before UA. As a result, the requirements and specification phases became less formal and less rigorous. Users and testers began being involved earlier and earlier in the implementation process.

As computer projects became more user-centered (less paycheck generators used by "computer operators" and more information systems used by office workers) and computers became more common (fewer giant mainframes, often in another town and more desktop computers) non-programmers became more common in large projects and non-programmers became less common in small projects. The myth of the programmer in the basement was born, as well as the myth of the super-programmer who understands the technology and problem domain and user experience and maintenance issues and the marketing. The super-programmer was the software architect, the designer, the Supreme Software Being.

In direct opposition to the perceived tyranny of the super-programmer, the agile paradigm was created to solve the problem of the central designer: the central, hierarchical designer could be a bottleneck and could be out of touch with changing requirements and shifting priorities. More on agile below.

These transitions are not smooth or swift: the leading edge and the trailing edge are often both common during transitions. These transitions often start in academia and work their way out from the academy into the workplace. So it was possible for a programmer to have to be conversant with multiple paradigms, each paired with specific development environments.

Once you have your requirements and your specification, you need a design that will satisfy those requirements and follow that specification.

TOP-DOWN

The top-down paradigm starts with a high-level breakdown of the technology to be created. Famously associated with block diagrams and iteration. Top-down is also deeply entwined with the levels of abstraction (each block in the diagram can be thought of as a level of abstraction which is broken down further in another diagram).

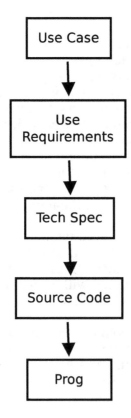

As one breaks down the blocks into sub-blocks, the iterations produce an ever-lower level of abstraction and an ever-greater level of detail. This is why some people consider this paradigm to be "stepwise refinement."

This approach really suits the way some people think. This approach is also really jarring to some people. There are many academic critiques of this approach. I will not attempt one here. But top-down is definitely a concept a good programmer should be aware of and, whatever its merits or demerits, top-down is still in use today and sometimes you will be forced to use it whether you like it or not and whether or not you personally enjoy it.

BOTTOM-UP

The bottom-up paradigm starts with defined pieces and considers how best to assemble them into a whole which means the requirements. Web pages are often the result of bottom-up design: you take the various elements defined by HTML and then build larger elements from the low-level elements and then build pages out of the larger elements.

Bottom-up is the obvious choice if the basic framework is already set. I would argue that using Ruby-on-Rails is often an exercise in bottom-up design since that environment has such strong opinions about how Web pages are constructed and about how Web apps should work, internally.

Bottom-up is also often written up in academic circles, and bottom-up is often compared and contrasted with top-down. In fact, Wikipedia has just such an entry:

```
en.wikipedia.org/wiki/Top-down_and_bottom-up_design
```

Just like top-down, bottom-up has both its proponents and detractors, but the fact remains that bottom-up really suits some people and seems natural to them and trying to force them to use some other methodology can be a really bad idea.

OOD

Object orientation can either be a software design paradigm or a programming paradigm, so we will discuss it under both rubrics.

Object Orientated Design (OOD) is the practice of drawing hard boundaries around the building blocks of your design (or implementation) and treating those building blocks as though they were physical blocks. The data and the code are packaged up into objects which are only accessible via specified "methods" (procedures or functions) and "attributes" (data elements associated with the object).

One of the greatest strengths of OOD is the effective hiding of data and code. Functionality and data elements are "exposed" only through the well-defined object methods and attributes. This cuts way down on the use of side-effects and other risky programming practices.

OOD is generally considered to be boon to maintenance and support staff. OOD is also a terrific fit for the way some people think; and for programmers who use Object Oriented Programming (OOP), OOD is either a great boon or a tempting prejudice. But OOD is still alive and kicking so a good programmer has to know what it is, its strengths and its weaknesses.

As a design paradigm, OOD is very close to bottom-up: bottom-up gives us a list of functional units which translate very well into "objects."

AGILE

The unofficial motto of the agile paradigm is "move fast and break stuff." This is saner than it sounds because it is a reaction to the notoriously long lead time to get the traditional, monolithic, designer-centered approach.

The hallmark of agile paradigm is the cross-functional team with a programmer, a project manager, a stakeholder and sometimes a support person. The idea is to break down tasks into their smallest chunks and then turn a large number of agile teams loose to take those small steps. In theory, the team has all the decision-making it needs, so there is less overhead and less hand-wringing and more forward progress.

(I am less clear on how the stuff that you are breaking is designed and built in the first place: I have only ever come into the agile process after the initial development.)

Fast, Easy, Maintainable

Once you have a design, of whatever type and whatever level of detail, it is time to start developing software.

In my experience, software development has these dimensions:

TIME NEEDED TO COMPLETE

Writing, debugging and deploying software can be fast or slow, often tied to the attributes of the development environment and to how well the development environment suits the task.

EFFORT NEEDED TO WRITE

Writing, debugging and deploying software can be painful or easy, often tied to the attributes of the development environment and to how well the development environment suits the task.

MAINTENANCE BURDEN

Keeping a software system running and current can be harder or easier, depending on many factors, but development environment is often the determining factor.

REAL-LIFE VALUE JUDGEMENTS

The good news is that it is a very rare project that requires optimization along all three of these dimensions. Are you banging out a tool to help in support or debugging? Then Time and Effort are likely your priorities. Are you creating a product you plan to sell and support for a long time? Then Effort and Maintenance are probably your priorities.

What Kind of Team?

The kind of development team you have is an important factor in choosing a programming language and development environment.

Small teams have fewer resources, but fewer points of confusion, fewer moving parts and, as a colleague of mine once said, "delightfully short lines of communication." Small teams are easier to keep on the same page, but small teams are generally under pressure to be productive, to be quick and to make things easy. Small teams tend to pick a powerful, high-level programming language and all use it. Often small teams also use a bottom-up approach, to exploit the rich set of intrinsics that high-level development environments usually offer.

Large teams have more resources, but more points of confusion, more moving parts and sometimes rather long lines of communication. Large teams can have sub-teams with different skills and possibly even different development environments. Large teams can use low-level programming languages which allow greater specificity in what you build but more work to build it.

OOP

As discussed in the OOD section, object orientation can either be a software design paradigm or a programming paradigm. Object-oriented Programming (OOP) does not need to rely on the environment to enforce OOP but generally if you are into OOP then you are into OOP environments. Ruby can support objects, but does not need to. C++ is heavily oriented toward objects.

OOP can look like a religion from the outside: it has avid devotees and bitter detractors. In my experience OOP has some real strengths and real drawbacks. With a large team, OOP helps keep the lines of responsibility clean and enforced. With small teams, OOP helps keep the eyes on the prize, helps focus the team on the design.

As I have noted in every other section, OOP really fits the way some people think. Trying to change their mind about this is generally a mutually-irritating waste of time. A good program can roll with OOP even it is not her natural way of thinking, because programming paradigms are not religions. Use the good ones where they are a good fit. Roll with it if someone forces one on you: determine its strengths and weaknesses and exploit the former and avoid being stung by the latter.

Roll Your Own

One of the reasons to learn about formal languages and compilers and interpreters is that formal languages make good interfaces to technology, which is why we have computer programming languages in the first place.

But we also have lots of formal languages that we use to create computer applications: SQL, XML, HTML, HL7 and SGML to name a few. There are application configuration languages, like YAML. Many embedded devices have a command line interpreter (CLI) as an interface with a simple command language to give the user access to the device's functionality. For what is a set of commands for a device if not an interpreted computer language?

If you create technology that is complex to use, then you might want to consider a layered approach: a command language at the lowest level, for experts and debugging, and then one or more user interfaces which are thin wrappers on that low level.

Writing compilers and interpreters is not a dark art: it is branch of computing which need not remain a mystery. *Writing Compilers & Interpreters* (An Applied Approach) by Ronald Mak is a great place to start.

Sense of Scope

One of the most important things a programmer needs to know is when his or her approach is a bad fit; in other words, when a task is taking too long, or a task is harder than it should be. Before you start, make an honest assessment as to how hard and how long and commit to it, perhaps in an email to yourself or by mentioning it to another human being. Once you start a task it is all too easy to lose perspective and to let yourself believe that every delay and every detour is excusable.

Once you realize that you are going down a rat hole, you need a new approach. If you don't have a Plan B, then this self-awareness will not be helpful. The more you know, the more options you have when you hit a brick wall.

Delve Deeper, Chapter 5

1. What is the difference between a language and a notation?

2. Is Sign Language a natural language, or a formal language, or a way of encoding a particular natural language?

3. Is music a formal language or a notation or both or neither?

4. Look up the natural language "Linear B"; is it a language or a notation?

5. Create a family tree for ANSI C, C++, Java and Javascript.

6. Do the five W's for your favourite programming language; for your least favourite.

7. Want to know more about compiling? **Compilers** by Aho, Sethi & Ullman, subtitled "Principles, Techniques, and Tools" and also called "the dragon book." The book is not new but it is a classic and it is holding up pretty well.

8. Searching for "programming languages by type" in Wikipedia.

9. Find discussions of programming languages and their relationship to "strong" and "weak" typing in Wikipedia and elsewhere.

10. Look up side-effects in the programming context and figure out what is good about them and what is bad, with reference to the Fast, Easy and Maintainable framework.

11. Look up lexical scoping and figure out how your favorite development environment handles lexical scoping.

12. Check out **The Art of War** by Sun Tzu. Programming is war: the war between the abstract and the concrete.

13. See if you can find Dan Ariely's TED talk entitled **What Makes Us Feel Good About Our Work**

Operating Systems

This chapter is about Operating Systems (O/S for short). It is not intended as an introduction to any specific O/S but rather an introduction to the idea of the O/S in general. The O/S is something every kind of programmer needs to understand in order to write better software.

In my mind, an operating system (O/S) is software that controls the various resources present in a typical computer system: the CPU, the RAM, the hard disk, the I/O subsystem, and whatever else might in the hardware package.

O/S Concepts

In order to talk about operating systems in general and particular operating systems in specific, we need to define some terms.

System versus User

Remember that in this context "user" means "human using the O/S" and *not* "human using a piece of application software." In the O/S domain, there is the "user" and there is the "system." So when we talk about the O/S, we talk of system software, system interfaces, etc. When we talk applications, we talk of application software, application interfaces (APIs), etc. For example, when we talk about how much of the CPU's attention a process uses, we talk of both its user time (time spent in user software) and system time (time spent in system software). Effectively, user time is usually elapsed time and system time is how much of that elapsed time the CPU was devoted to the software.

Foreground versus Background

A concept closely related to the system versus user duality is the foreground verus background dichotomy. In some operating systems (Unixoid ones in particular) the space in which processes run is divided into the foreground and the background. The foreground is the user space; processes in the foreground get input from the keyboard or mouse, they are allowed to send output to the console or the screen. The background is the system space; processes in the background are either suspended or running. Running in the background usually means running without direct user input. The background is generally where software services run: email servers, web servers and other services. The O/S itself runs helper processes in the background: the file system, the I/O system and so on.

Multi-Tasking

The modern O/S offers support for what is now called "multi-tasking." Before this term leaked into common parlance to mean "humans juggling multiple points of focus" it was a technical term meaning an O/S which was able to have its host computer's CPU switch execution contexts so quickly that multiple processes seemed to be executing at the same time. Literally, of course, a single CPU can only execute one instruction at a time and that instruction can only come from one executable image at a time. But processes often get "blocked," particularly on I/O, as they wait for input from a keyboard or a NIC or some other device, or as they wait for an output to be successfully accepted by the output device (for example, waiting for a hard disk to finish a request to write data).

(I will leave the very complicated case of computers with multiple CPUs to the future, perhaps ever a class you take in college with someone who is better versed in this topic than I am.)

Since processes tend to get hung up on I/O, especially when considering the computer's operation at the speeds at which CPUs operate, there is no reason not "swap out" a blocked process in favor of an unblocked process--assuming that time required for of this "context switch" is not so great as to dwarf the expected wait.

However, we should never forget that multi-tasking is a mirage: it is a terrific thing when it works but, as the engineers like to say, its failure mode is not graceful. When it goes wrong, it goes very wrong. The computer appears to lock up. Determining which requests will be satisfied and which will be lost, let alone in what order those lucky requests will be satisfied, is mind-bendingly difficult. Often there is no hope for it but to abandon all currently in-process work and reboot.

This is not a common experience anymore, except in the Web Server domain. In the old days, we would use multi-user systems and watch in helpless horror as the bad judgement of one user in launching a task or tasks which was too much for the O/S to handle. The system would appear to be utterly unresponsive but, alas! all too often our keystrokes were going into a queue somewhere and suddenly, some subset of them would be processed. We would watch in horror as random keys we hit in frustration suddenly were faithfully processed.

These days the "many users at once" mirage most often breaks down when many users hit the same web server at the same time and then performance quickly degrades from mediocre to terrible to unusable. The standard cure for this problem is shutting down the web server and restarting it.

Terminals

Terminus literally means "end point." Something is "terminal" when it is an end point. A computer terminal is a devices which combine a display device and an input device, almost always via a serial cable and serial communications hardware on either end.

Originally terminals were based on typewriters: the output was a stream of perforated paper pages and the input was a keyboard. The good news was that the paper gave us a persistent record of the session which was legible even if the computer was down. The bad news was that the teletype was noisy and slow and was not a very capable display device: it was the ultimate line-at-a-time technology.

Then came the "glass tty" which substituted a screen for the paper, but kept the keyboard. The shift to a Cathode Ray Tube (CRT) enabled the "full-screen" era: you can clear the screen, you can have forms which can be filled in, and had the ability to move the cursor around the screen. The classic "dumb ASCII terminal" was the DEC VT100 (we will encounter the Digital Equipment Corporation below).

(Confusing as it was, the advent of the PC meant that we could have a PC run software to emulator a terminal: the terminal emulator. This was confusing because you were using a computer running an O/S to run software which acted like a dumb ASCII terminal.)

After the terminal emulator arrived, replacing the slow-but-reliable serial connection was replaced by a network connection thanks to the then-revolutionary *telnet* program which was developed in the late 1960s and everywhere by the early 1970s.

Brace yourself, this gets pretty complicated pretty quickly: this is how, in 1982, you would have seen me using a dumb ASCII terminal to talk to a local Unix host as a user. One of the processes I would have been running would have been telnet which allowed my session to pretend to be a terminal, which terminal session was connected to my physical terminal but the other end of the telnet session was a remote Unix host whose physical location was immaterial so long as the network connection was up. My keystrokes travelled to that remote host over the network and that remote host's responses coming back to me over the network. The assumption was the the network was private, since Internet connections were slow and expensive and we only used them when we had to.

By the early 2000s, the Secure Shell (ssh) came along to replace the oh-so-useful telnet, to add the layer of security that telnet lacks.

Kernel

The core, the center, the innermost part of an O/S is called "the kernel" by analogy with a grass grain such as wheat.

The kernel has to be fast, efficient and effective. Everybody wants the O/S to work as quickly as possible but to never make mistakes, or get hung up or crash. An app is only as good as the kernel upon which it rests.

The kernel hacker is a special breed. They have to be great coders and hardware mavens and software architects. Linux owes its existence to one such hacker: originally, Linux was a kernel which used all the public-domain drivers and other system software which had been written for Unix.

Unix may have been developed by AT&T, but it was also heavily contributed to by the University of California at Berkeley. We used to say Unix and Berkeley Unix. Since Berkeley had many hackers and few dollars, Berkeley contributed many drivers and other software designed to run with the Unix kernel. So there was lots of what we would now call "open source" Unix software but no environment on which to run that software. Once Linus Torvalds created the first Linux kernel, suddenly there was a Linux distribution: a free operating system that actually worked. It worked well. It was good. In 1992, I got a copy and installed it on an unneeded PC. I had a fully-featured Unix environment in my office, without the high cost of server hardware and the high cost of an AT&T Unix license. I knew that my professional world had changed forever. I installed my first Linux-based the next year.

File Systems

Hard drives are generally big and slow, especially when compared to RAM.

Usually we use a file system (sometimes written "F/S") to put files on hard drives. The typical file system has a very layered architecture:

1. Hardware; the spinning magnetic disks or whatever stores the data.

2. Block-level I/O: disk controllers, at their lowest level, read and write data in blocks. When I started out, blocks were 256 bytes big but soon they were 512 bytes big and then 1024 bytes big and then 2048 and then 4096 and then.... Buffering usually happens at the block-level.

3. File-level I/O: on-disk structures which keep track of all the files and all their attributes and all the directories.

File systems organize those files in directories. File systems read and write data from and to a storage device in units which are measured in the "cluster size."

Files are a name associated with a linked list of clusters. If the cluster size is small, the file system can store small files efficiently. If the cluster size is large, the File system access large files efficiently.

Aside from the storage space / access time dilemma, there are other considerations:

SPACE EFFICIENT

Some file systems are designed to be space-efficient, to store files with a minimum amount wasted disk space. These are often highly "tuneable" so you can set the cluster size (and other parameters) to best suit your particular situation. Web servers are often tuned to efficiently store small files because HTML documents are usually small.

TIME EFFICIENT

Some file systems are designed to be time-efficient, to serve up the contents of files as quickly as possible. Buffering is key in these file systems.

FAULT TOLERANT

Some file systems are designed to be fault-tolerant, which means that they can recover from a limited amount of data loss: hardware failure or software failure or user error.

UPDATES

Some file systems are designed to handle lots of I/O, to support a high volume of data changes: inserting data into files, changing existing data in files, delete data from files, as well as creating new files and deleting old ones at the directory level.

RAW DEVICES

For those of us who worked in databases, files were a luxury we could not afford. We used what were called "raw devices" which were "files" which stopped at the block-level. The file systems treated the raw device as a fixed array of blocks. No buffering, no directories, no file overhead: just blocks.

We made our database system (yes, people used to write their own database systems) block-based as well. The records were packed into the blocks and the blocks read and written as units.

The lack of a file system greatly improved performance. But raw devices were rather...inconvenient. You could not simply copy or rename or delete the files. You had to write software to read each block, in order, and then write each block to a tape drive or back up device yourself.

HAVING IT ALL

As CPUs became bigger (more bits) and faster (more instructions per second) and hard drives became bigger (more bytes) and faster (more bytes in or out per second), file systems became more complex and more sophisticated.

Buffering has become quite sophisticated. Tuning has gotten better and better. Now you can often have good performance and decent space efficiency and dependable fault tolerance. For many applications, you can have it all.

At some point, in the early 1990s, we found that one of our clients had fiddled with one of our old apps. Their programmers had removed most of our application-level buffering which should have made the performance pretty bad, but it was *better* without our in-app buffering. File system buffering had improved so much in the intervening several years that our buffering was hurting instead of helping. It was hurting because unneeded buffering is just useless overhead.

Real-Time O/S

All that buffer is awesome if a system is being used by lots of people, or lots of processes or for many purposes. But what if you want the lowest possible real-world elapsed time, not a compromise between system time and user time? What if the computer is dedicated to a critical task such as landing an airplane or controlling a space shuttle or calculating optimal paths for a fleet of oil tankers as they span the globe.

If you have a specialized task, then the buffering, even smart buffering, will hurt more than it helps. You can turn off the buffering in a modern, interactive O/S which will help a bit but even better is an O/S without the buffering in the first place. We call such an O/S a "real-time O/S" (RTOS) because processes tend to happen in real time.

Mainframes are also well-suited to the tasks that benefit from a RTOS, but mainframes are very, very expensive to own and operate and a dedicated mainframe is even more so. So a cheaper computer running an RTOS is often the right choice for critical tasks which must be executed as quickly as possible.

Booting

In some ways, the kernel is just a piece of software running on the hardware in a very privileged space. In other ways, the kernel is unlike any other software: it is the software that runs software, the process that spawns processes, the environment that is the basis for the environment.

Booting is how the kernel gets up and running. Every computer system needs a default output device and a default input device so that the booting process can be controlled, if need be, by a human. Before the PC and its close relative, the workstation, the default output device and the default input device were the same device: the console, which was a terminal that was blessed by virtue of being connected directly to the system unit via a serial port..

Multi-user systems usually boot into single-use mode, in which only the console is "live" which means that only the console is being scanned for input and output is only being sent to the console.

Batch versus Interactive

In general, an O/S is either aimed at efficient processing (batch) or aimed at human interaction (interactive).

Batch software is geared toward processing input into output, generally without human intervention. Mainframes were originally almost completely batch-oriented (now they have had some interactive bells and whistles added to them, but not many).

Interactive software is geared toward interaction with human users; smart phones are almost completely interactive.

BATCH

Batch O/Ses run jobs. A job generally defines four things:

1. The Input: a file or files or tape drive or card reader)

2. The Process: software to run with this input

3. The Output: when to put the processes output

4. The Errors: optionally, you could capture errors and other diagnostic output

Jobs went into a queue, which is a fancy British term for "line" as in "wait in line." Just like a line of people waiting for service, a job queue is a line of jobs waiting for their turn to run.

Technically, a queue is a simple data structure which keeps its elements in the order in which they were submitted; further, a queue only allows you to add to the tail and take from the head. We say that a queue is a "first in, first out" or FIFO data structure. (Just as an orderly and fair line of people should be.)

The batch O/S generally plodded along, taking jobs from the queue in the order in which those jobs had been submitted for execution. To "run" a job, its definition was taken out of the queue and that definition was used to set up a session and then the associated software was executed with the output being captured to wherever was specified and errors saved wherever was specified.

Jobs returned a return code; all too often, the job "abended" which meant that the job experienced an ABnormal END; if you did not capture the error output, all you had was a error code in the return code.

The typical batch O/S generally had a rather simple (some would say "brutal" or "simple") user interface (UI) because the goal is to run jobs and not to interact with humans.

INTERACTIVE

Interactive O/Ses interact with users. Their priority is generally user input. They generally run user-oriented apps, such as spreadsheets or word-processors, which primarily accept user input in the foreground.

In the beginning, interactive systems could only be interacted with using terminals, then terminal emulators, then networked terminal sessions, then secure shell (SSH) sessions.

What all these interaction modes have in common is the transmission of characters, usually generated by a keyboard. Sure, some of the characters where not really characters, such as "form feed" (better know as "clear screen") or "tab" or various "special characters" which allowed software to position the cursor on the screen. We called the UIs built on top of the character stream "character-based user interfaces."

Then, in 1984, the mighty X-windows hit the scene. It allowed Unixoid systems to provide a true Graphical User Interface (GUI) to apps. X-windows terminals were a thing, but mostly what I saw were workstations and PC running the display side of the X-windows protocol.

Shortly thereafter, in 1985, the world's first Microsoft Windows version was released, which seemed rather like a window-based MS-DOS extension.

Not long after that, a trouble joint project between IBM and Microsoft, OS/2, which was supposed to be the next big thing in PC operating systems. The market had other ideas and OS/2 never took off.

The march toward our current situation, in which there seems to be only two mainstream O/S options: either the Windows family of operating systems or the Unix family of operating systems.

Computer Environment Evolution

We are going to take another trip down memory lane because, as Shakespeare wrote, "past is prologue" and the traces of what went before are still there in today's O/Ses.

This is why MS-DOS has "batch" files, with their ".bat" extension. This is why Unix and Linux have terminals and pseudo-terminals and why Unixoid systems use the abbreviation "tty" even though teletype terminals are long gone. This is why Windows development environments and Java have the concepts of a "console."

When computer use exploded in the 1970s and 1980s, there were many different brands and sizes of computer and each had its own environment: the mainframe, the minicomputer, the microcomputer, the super mini and finally the Personal Computer (PC) and workstation.

Mainframe

International Business Machines (IBM) ruled the mainframe market with their 360 series. Each of their O/S options from this era were very batch job oriented:

• Conversational Monitor System (CMS)

• Time Share Options (TSO)

Minicomputer

Digital Equipment Corporation (DEC) ruled the minicomputer market with their VAX line which came after their breakthrough microcomputer PDP-11 and its variants. Their PDP-11 was one of most popular hosts for the Unix operating system

• Virtual Memory System (VMS)

• Unix

Microcomputer

DEC's PDP-11 was the archetypal microcomputer and its popularity helped make the Internet possible (email, etc). Unix was born for the PDP-11 and much of the Internet infrastructure was written on PDP-11s: email, ftp, WAIS and others.

However, once the VAX came along, Unix was hurriedly upgraded from a 16-bit operating system to a 32-bit operating system with backward compatibility. So in my first job out of college, our PDP-11 ran Venix which was a true 16-bit O/S and not a 32-bit O/S which worked well enough on 16-bit machines. Backward compatibility is rarely as good as you would hope.

Minix

The first car engine I ever looked at was the engine of a 1969 Dodge Dart. That engine was a beast. That engine was simple. That engine was dependable. That engine was clear and simple to follow: the parts were obvious and clear.

The last car engine I ever seriously examined was in a 1989 Honda Civic. That engine was tiny, efficient, modular and electronic. The components were sealed in cases I could not tell their true shape. The components had sub-components which optimized its functions. I recognized very little. I still understood the basic layout but I was hazy on the Electronic Fuel Injection instead of a carburetor, the on-board computer instead of a timing belt, etc.

So I imagine it must be for a young programmer these days, whose first kernel is the Linux kernel. The Linux kernel is a beast. It is complicated. It is refined. It is difficult to follow.

If you want start with the O/S equivalent of a 1969 Dodge Dart, I highly recommend *Operating Systems* (Design And Implementation) by the great Andrew S. Tanenbaum. In it he describes Minix, a Unixoid O/S which predated Linux by many years whose purpose in life was less to be an O/S and more to teach students about how an O/S is designed and implemented.

MINIX took off after Tanenbaum's work on it stopped and it is now a full-blown O/S, but MINIX 1.0 is still a great way to find out more if you are interested in what goes on under the hood in an O/S.

```
https://en.wikipedia.org/wiki/MINIX
```

Running Program (O/S)

Let us return to our usual starting point, a running program.

In this context, O/Ses, a running program is a process. A process is an O/S structure which allows an O/S to keep track of a runable program, to allow it to move the process to the foreground or the background, to suspend the process, to hook up the input and output, to support security policies and enforce permissions and finally to terminate the program.

In order to run a program, you had to log in. In order to log in, the kernel had to spawn a login process, accept and verify your credentials and then establish your user context (home directory, user ID, etc), spawn a shell or command line interpreter (CLI).

Once you were logged in, and your keyboard is the input to a shell and your display is the output of that shell, you are ready to run a program.

You asked the shell to run a program by giving it a file name which contained a runable program. The shell used the kernel's process subsystem to spawn a process and the file system to get the program's executable contents and the kernel's process management to start up that process and voila! A running program.

Delve Deeper, Chapter 6

1. Search for the IBM document "What is TSO?" to see that batch-oriented computer survives to this day.

2. Figure out what Wide Area Information Servers (WAIS) were for and why the World Wide Web killed WAIS.

3. Find out what you can about HAL/S.

4. Compare the Linux ext2 file system and Reiser file system.

5. How does NFS work? Why would anyone use it?

Data Structures

This chapter is about data structures, by which we mean ways to organize data, either in RAM or on disk (and how the two are very different).

What Are They For?

Data structures allow us to associate various data elements together into logical units. Data structures often correspond to real-world objects, but not always.

In a practical sense, data structures exist to support a certain programming task or tasks. If a data structure does not make your life easier then you did not do a good job designing it.

RAM Data Structures

RAM is easy and quick to access. In nearly every environment, RAM is much scarcer than disk space. RAM objects are easy to link together because memory addresses are easy to manipulate.

Since loading data into RAM takes effort, programmers usually process the data as they load it, so RAM structures are generally more complicated than disk data structures and RAM structures are often part of more complicated meta structures, or structures-within-structures.

Disk Data Structures

Disk is hard and relatively slow to access. In nearly every environment, disk is much more plentiful than RAM.

Since storing data on disk is relatively slow, programmers usually process the data as they store it, so disk structures are generally simpler and smaller than RAM structures.

In the database context, data is generally stored in fields which are part of records.

Common Uses

In so very many cases, RAM and disk data structures are used in this way:

1. Read the data off the disk

2. Process the data into a RAM structure

3. Manipulate the data in software

4. Write the changed data out of the RAM onto disk

Links

Before we talk about links, let us consider what it is that links link together.

TREES & NODES

A common data structure is the "tree" which is so called because this data structure is mapped out as a diagram, it somewhat resembles an upside-down tree. "Tree" is usually short for "binary search tree."

The units which make up a tree are called "nodes." Once you put the nodes into a tree, you can "traverse" the tree in order to access the nodes in sorted order, as we will see later under searching and sorting.

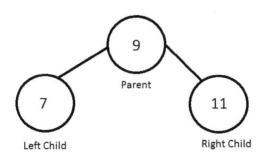

Binary Search Tree [1]

ELEMENTS & LISTS

Lists and arrays are made up of elements. As we will see below, if you want to access data in sorted order and there are not that many elements (data points), you can put them into a linked list of either the singly-linked or doubly-linked variety.

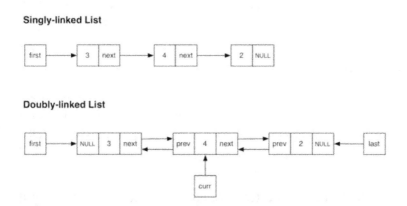

Linked Lists [2]

ARRAYS

Arrays are so common that we forget how pretty darn cool they are. You give them a simple numeric index, they give you a data element.

Consider the array diagrammed below: it is named "a" (presumably for for "array") and has five elements, all of which are small integers: 1, 2, 4, 8 and 16.

1	a[0]
2	a[1]
4	a[2]
8	a[3]
16	a[4]

Arrays [3]

LINKING

Data structures are often linked together into larger structures: nodes linked into trees, elements linked into lists, array members linked into arrays, keys linked to data in hashes.

These links can be either be low level ("hard") or high level ("soft").

HARD LINKS

Hard links get you directly to the object; by "directly" mostly I mean via the environment, via a system call or system intrinsic. In other words, following a hard link requires no programming in the app.

In the RAM context, a hard link is a memory address, also known as "pointer." Every programming environment that allows pointer manipulation has a "get the address of" function to support linking.

In the disk context, a hard link comes down to an offset and length inside a file. With an offset and a length, you can ready the object off the disk in a single system "read" call.

SOFT LINKS

Soft links get you to the object via data values instead of pointers. This can be done directly or indirectly. By "directly" I mean by scanning the two data structures and comparing the values. By "indirectly" I mean in a two-step process using a key value:

1. Find the key value in an index; finding a value in a sorted list is called "looking up" the value and software which does this job is called a "look up."

2. Get the hard link out of the index.

A hash works this way. An SQL key works this way. A classic index works this way.

PROS & CONS

Hard links are faster to chase to the actual object ("dereference") but more work to maintain and brittle like glass, by which I mean they break if the structure changes.

Soft links are slower to dereference but less work to maintain and ductile like gold, by which I mean they work unless the key values change on either end.

As computer power and RAM and disk space have grown more plentiful, the trend has been toward soft links: many run-time environments have the soft link dereferencing built-in and many host systems have enough power to run a soft link-based system with more than acceptable performance.

A Great Data Structures Book

I am about to recommend yet another book for extended reading, so here is a quick side-note on why I keep recommending books despite living in the Information Age:

1. These books are generally old enough that they are still general. They don't assume that the world's only programming language is C. Or Java. Or Python. Or Ruby. Or any particular language. Most of these books do not assume that programmers are one-programming-language programmers.

2. These books are generally not tied to a single O/S or development environment for very similar reasons.

3. These books are physical books, so you can't easily skim them, or search them or sample them. You pretty much have to read them, old school as that may be.

The book is *Data Structures And Algorithms* by Aho, Hopcroft & Ullman. It presents some common data structures in the context of the algorithms they support. Reading it should give you sense of the relationship of data structures to programming, and vice versa. If you put in the effort, your reward will be a deeper understanding of how common jobs are done and how the complexity is divided between data structure and code.

Some Examples

Here are some common data structures you should already know or should be able to find.

EMAIL

An email is a data structure, in the "structured text" vein. Email is data structure where much of the complexity was shifted from the data structure and onto the software. The data structure is deliberately very simple and lightly structured. Loading email off of disk and into RAM is very easy. Writing email to disk from RAM is very easy. Sending email across a write is easy. In this case, it was a solid choice to keep the data structure simple and to make it almost identical between RAM and disk.

SQL TABLE

An SQL table is a disk structure highly optimized for reading and writing on a disk, to minimize disk I/O. An SQL table is a complex data structure, a contain which can contain binary integers, floating point numbers, dates, date times, text, or some combination thereof.

SQL ROW

The in-memory representation of a row from an SQL table is optimized for processing in RAM. A row is a complicated structure which links together structures which represent fields. The fields often have more than just a value attribute; they have permissions and user-level locking and a host administrative tasks to support.

Algorithms For Data Structures

There are well-defined tools in the data manipulator's tool kit that every aspiring bit-basher should master.

Translation

I would have preferred to go through these concepts in order from simplest to most complex, but the common use (and misuse) of the term "translation" means that I have to deal with "translation" first.

Everyone has an idea of what translation entails, but actually defining it is harder than one might expect.

First, it is time to introduce a jargon term I will need: semantics. Roughly, "semantics" are what a linguistic unit means, the payload of a linguistic construct. Consider the semantics of these statements:

• The New York Yankees rule.

• I am a baseball fan; specifically, I follow the Yankees.

• Yanks, yo!

• There are many baseball teams in the United States: the Yankees and some others.

Language is tricky: there are more components than semantics involved in linguistic expressions: tone, overtone, subtext. When we say "translate" we rarely specify to what degree we care about non-semantic elements.

To translate a linguistic element requires the following steps:

1. Accept input in the source language system.

2. Determine the semantics of the input.

3. Encode those semantics in the target language.

The second step is a doozy. Technically, only people can translate since only people experience "meaning" and only linguistic units can be translated, only inputs which can be comprehended by people can be translated.

But such hyper-correctness is not why we are here: we are because the term "translate" in this context often has "mechanical" implied. "Mechanical translation" is done by machines. Mechanical translation is about identifying the underlying semantics and associating the different expressions at the semantic level.

Mercifully we are not talking about the translation of semantics from one natural language to another; here we are talking about translating data (our semantics) from one data structure to another, by way of an intermediate format.

Frequently computer programmers are asked to move data (configurations, email addresses, etc) from one application to another. In real terms, this means from the source app's data structures to the target app's data structures. A common mistake is to try to move the data in a single step; if the two data structures are different enough, the effort to move from one to the other is so much harder than it has to be. (By the way, trying to do it in one step is "transliteration" which will be discussed in the next section.

To translate the data from the source to the target, you need an intermediate format which is our equivalent of "meaning." I, myself, favor the MUMPS format: all text, line-oriented, with the following simple structure:

```
field_name=value
```

For example:

```
name=Bruce Wayne
address=Wayne Manor
city=Gotham
state=New York
country=USA
```

So when I move data from one app to another, I use the classic translation method:

1. Define a simple export format, easy to output, easy to input.

2. Export the data from the source into the intermediate format.

3.   Import the data from the intermediate format into the target.

Sometimes I get lucky and the source app has an export format and the target app has an input format and all I need to do reformat the input into the output (technically, "transformation" as we will see below).

But either way, it is often much easier to several small programs than one big one. It may feel better to slog through a single mono-lith but a professional should do the most reliable, fastest, most maintainable solution.

☺ (By the way, this is the Unix philosophy: a figurative strand of pears, a literal chain of filters hooked together with the output of one small program being the input of the next small program.) ☺

Consider translation from computer language source code to ma-chine code: that is a complicated process. Consider transliteration from macro assembler to machine code: that is a simple process.

Transliteration

Transliteration is the simple substitution of one thing for another. Transliteration can be accomplished with a keyed array (also called a "hash") or a pair of arrays.

Having spent so many hours using either the CLI for Unix or the one for MS-DOS, I have memorize the transliteration of some ba-sic commands:

```
+------------------+--------+------+
| Command          | MS-DOS | Unix |
+------------------+--------+------+
| File Copy        | COPY   | cp   |
+------------------+--------+------+
| Print a file     | PRINT  | lp   |
+------------------+--------+------+
| Rename a file    | RENAME | mv   |
+------------------+--------+------+
| Delete a file    | DEL    | rm   |
+------------------+--------+------+
```

```
| List files        | DIR    | ls   |
+-------------------+--------+------+
| Change directory  | CD     | cd   |
+-------------------+--------+------+
```

Transliteration is great when the job requires nothing more, but that is not often the case. Transliteration with a little bit of preprocessing or postprocessing is fine. Transliteration as a small of a sprawling, complicated, special-case ridden mess is a warning sign that you probably should use one of the other methods.

Transduction

Many moons ago, I was taught that transduction is a technique which shuffles the input components around without changing them. I cannot seem to find this definition on the web, so perhaps my professor was off in his own little world. But the concept has served me so well for so many years that I will risk perpetrating an error and repeat the definition here.

Here are some examples from natural language:

```
Input: He is the greatest of all men!
Output: Of all men, he is the greatest!

Input: Ice cream is a delicious dessert.
Output: A delicious dessert is ice cream.

Input: Able was I ere I saw Elba
Output: I was able ere I saw Elba

Input: Be a Jedi, yes you will
Output: Yes, you will be a Jedi
```

I have used this technique to process data many times because it is a compromise between simple transliteration and full translation. If the difference between the input and the output is mostly in order or hierarchy, then transliteration is too little and translation is too much: transduction to the rescue!

Note that I wrote "hierarchy": in a tree or some other kind of hierarchy, you can use transduction to "promote" an element (move it up the hierarchy) or "demote" an element (move it down the hierarchy).

For example, I often have to move data between health information systems which store the same data but in different hierarchies. For example, some systems key their data primarily on the "encounter" with the patient:

```
Encounter
        Dates
        Patient
                Date of Birth
                Sex
        MD
        Labs
                Test 1
                Test 2
```

Other systems key their data primarily on the patient:

```
Patient
        Encounter
                Dates
                MD
                Labs
                        Test 1
                        Test 2
```

In this case, we can see that transliteration is too little and translation is too much.

As a matter of practicality, we might need to build an intermediate structure which helps us bridge the gap between two different data models.

COMPARING CPU TIME & RAM REQUIREMENTS

From a computer programmer perspective, transduction takes constant space (memory) and is a pretty light load on the CPU. Transliteration is also constant RAM and light CPU. But translation is a potential yawning pit into which CPU time and RAM can be poured.

Transformation

The same perhaps-insane professor claimed that "transformation" was a technique where there were clear rules to govern the data shuffling.

In our earlier example of Unix and MS-DOS commands, we did not cover file names and path separators. Specifically we did not cover how to avoid trying to map the file names and instead of mapping them, to change the path separators in those file names.

We can define a simple transformation to more fully handle the issues by defining a short rule set to apply in addition to the transliteration:

1. Map the commands from one set to the other by using the transliteration we defined above;

2. Keep the file names unmapped by assuming that all non-commands are file names.

3. Having identified the file names, transliterate the path separators (back-slash for MS-DOS, forward-slash for Unix)

Some examples:

```
+------------------+--------------------+------------------+
| Command          | MS-DOS             | Unix             |
+------------------+--------------------+------------------+
| File Copy        | COPY a.txt .\TMP   | cp a.txt ./tmp   |
+------------------+--------------------+------------------+
| Print a file     | PRINT a.txt        | lp a.txt         |
+------------------+--------------------+------------------+
```

```
| Rename a file    | RENAME a.txt b.txt | mv a.txt b.txt |
+------------------+--------------------+----------------+
| Delete a file    | DEL a.txt          | rm a.txt       |
+------------------+--------------------+----------------+
| List files       | DIR                | ls             |
+------------------+--------------------+----------------+
| Change directory | CD .\TMP           | cd ./tmp       |
+------------------+--------------------+----------------+
```

Transformation is a very satisfying way to handle a wide variety of data processing tasks, especially tasks which involve tree manipulation. Specifically, I have done many jobs manipulating documents which were encoded as trees in structured text. Many XML documents whose document type definition had changed and which needed to be brought into compliance with the new document type definition.

Using editors to make changes like that is for people who do not know how to program.

Generate & Prune

Strange as it sounds. sometimes the best was to transform a data structure is to almost randomly shuffle the pieces and then see if the result of the shuffling passes the rules. In fact, you can "score" any given configuration and then choose the configuration with the highest score.

Software to shuffle the pieces around is pretty easy to write. Validating a configuration is not that hard. Often this approach is a much easier programming task then using rules to guide a transformation, but this approach requires much greater computing resources and an undeterminable amount of time.

Delve Deeper, Chapter 7

1. Design a linked list for a moderate number of lines from a text file. Write a program in the programming language of your choice to open a text file, read the lines into the list,

close the file and then print out the lines in reverse order.

2. Compare an address book entry from two different email clients.

3. Look up MUMPS, both the data format and the programming environment.

4. Work through an example of representing a data set first as SQL INSERT statements and second as an XML document. Which is better? Why?

Chapter 7 End Notes

[1] http://cppbetterexplained.com/binary-search-trees/

[2] http://codethataint.com/blog/linkedlist/

[3] http://www.fredosaurus.com/notes-cpp/arrayptr/array-diagrams.html

Databases

This chapter is about databases. It is likely that you are familiar with the abstract concept of "the data set" as well as the concrete reality of on-line databases.

Specifically, this chapter is about how data is organized on disk, in specialized formats we call "databases."

The DBMS

The software which manages the data in these formats is called "the database management system" or DBMS.

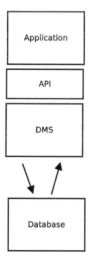

The DBMS has many jobs, but providing an interface to the database for applications is one of the most important and easily the most visible. The modern DBMS has been such a spectacular success that we take it for granted. If you are a programmer who needs to access or update a data set, you can just assume that there will be a DBMS and that using its API will be familiar and well-documented.

This success means that many programmers do not have to consider how efficiently a DBMS stores its data on disk. Most programmers do not have to consider how relatively fast a given DBMS is. It is assumed that whatever DBMS you have is efficient enough and fast enough.

One aspect of the DBMS that every programmer has to use in order to interact with the DBMS is the API.

These days, that API is almost always based on SQL. In fact SQL is so common as the basis of the DBMS API that a programmer can spend their entire career never using anything else.

The Database, Conceptually

Databases are, conceptually, a container data structure which organizes collections of different kinds of object into manageable units, usually files in the file system but no always. This aspect of databases is usually only of interest to database administrators rather than report programmers.

The objects in a database are fields, records and indices.

Fields, Records and Indices

Before we examine how a running program interacts with a DBMS, we need to take a quite detour to consider how a DBMS interacts with its database.

FIELDS

The earliest databases stored records which were containers for fields. Fields were completely analogous to variables in RAM: they had an offset, a length in bytes and a data type. Once a record was loaded into RAM, mapping a field to a variable was easy. Once the field was a variable, then software could read it, write it, modify it, clear it or set it. Once it had at least one changed field, the RAM version of the record was "dirty" and needed to be written out to disk. (In multi-user systems, the DBMS needed to know that the on-disk version was out-of-date so that other users wouldn't get out-of-date information when they tried to access that record.)

Fields can be NULL, which means "unset" in this context and "missing value" in the reporting context. In the integer context, NULL is often mistaken for zero, but NULL is not zero. In the string context, NULL is often mistaken for a string of zero length, but NULL is not a string of zero length.

RECORDS

Records were originally very basic data objects and we tended to force the data models of our apps to fit the simple record models; we tended to make very basic systems with a single data object. For example, lists of things (addresses, vinyl records, checks and deposits in a checkbook).

INDICES

In order to access records in some predetermined order, we used sorted lists of keys, usually with hard links to records. We called this sorted lists "indices" by analogy with analog indices: card indexes in libraries, the indices in the backs of books, etc.

Indices were expensive to maintain, both in terms of disk space and in terms of CPU time, so we tended to have the bare minimum number of them. The good news is that an index made accessing the records in a particular order very quick. The bad news is that accessing records in any other order took application code and

CPU time and RAM and therefore was hard to provide and slow to use.

(Remember the binary search tree in the data structures chapter? Indices were almost always in that format.)

SECONDARY RECORDS

When greater computing power made it possible, we added the concept of secondary records, which made the original records "primary" records and the "parent" of the secondary records. Secondary records held attributes about the primary record, or about the real-world thing which the primary record represented.

Ideally the secondary records held attributes which were optional, or repeated. Ideally the secondary records were linked together in addition to being linked to the primary record. The links were usually hard links. Sometimes the secondary records were linked in both directions, or "doubly linked."

SCHEMAS

The *structure* of a database is called "the schema." One of the cool things about SQL is that SQL has constructs which define the database structure. So an SQL schema can be processed by a DBMS, can be used by a DBMS to actually define a database. This means that an SQL export of a database can be self-descriptive, can actually define the database as well as the database.

CONFIGURATION

The allocation of records to files and directory path to the files and the permissions of users is called "the configuration."

Transaction Sets

In the early days of computerized business automation, much of the activity that we computerized were business transactions. Business automation was one of the first hot topics in computing, since businesses have money and computing was very expensive. We called this subfield "On-line Transaction Processing" or OLTP.

Business transactions were well-suited to being done by computers. Business transactions fit the query / response model. Business transactions were well-defined by businesses over years so that their employees could reliably execute them.

A "transaction set" is just what is sounds like: a group of transactions which go together, usually in a specific order. Typical examples include:

1. A deposit (so you have money)

2. A transfer (of the money you just deposited)

3. Another transfer

Here is another example:

1. Sell stock A, to get money

2. Buy stock B, as an investment

3. Transfer leftover money as profit

Usually, a transaction set was all-or-nothing: either do all of them, in order, or do none of them.

The cool part of making a set was not having to "back out" or "undo" if something went wrong; even cooler, the application programmer did not have to write error-handling code every time. The application programmer could depend on the DBMS which was presumably mature and reliable.

The not-cool part was having to have temporary data sets and to mix and match (check the production database but operate on the temporary one) and then apply all the transactions in the temporary database to the production database. Presumably all this hairy code worked, since it was part of the mature and reliable DBMS, but this still eats up RAM and disk space and creates a world of hurt if the system fails somehow during any of the production database updating.

There was also the problem that a naive application programmer might allow his or her application to create enormous transaction sets which required titanic temporary file space and humongous amounts of RAM and colossal amounts of CPU time. This was bad a scene, man, because when a transaction set fails, there is lots of cleaning up to do and when an enormous transaction set fails, there is enormously lots of cleaning up to do. Bad situations tend to get worse as the cleaning up of my enormous transaction set prevents the processing of your normal transaction set and users become baffled as to why reasonable transaction sets are suddenly failing.

Software Using Databases

From the beginning, there were two very different kinds of software which worked on databases: database loaders and database reports. Then loaders became importers and we added exporters. Then we found that we needed to back up database and restore them, and that users wanted to enter and view data directly, so UIs were born. That gave us the current slate:

1. Import (read an intermediate format, store as records)

2. Export (scan records, write out in intermediate format)

3. Back up (an export into a less general format with a selection generally based on when the data was last changed)

4. Restore (an import from a less general format, sometimes with a selection mechanism)

5. UIs (let users find, insert, edit or delete individual primary records and associated secondary records)

6. Reports (scan primary records and associated secondary records for the purpose of creating a formatted report: originally paper, then PDF and now often HTML)

These functions broke down into three basic categories: UIs, reports and database maintenance.

Database maintenance and UIs were quite specialized, but luckily you only needed a few of each. However, there never seemed to be enough report programmers.

We needed lots of report programmers and, in theory, they were easier to find than UI programmers or database programmers since in theory, they needed to have less specialized knowledge and perhaps even less programming ability.

In practice, in order to process a database to create a report, you often ended up needing to understand the database or risk having very slow reports. Worse, a badly written report could bring the system to its knees. Worst, a report which did not properly mirror the database structure and conventions might be just plain *wrong*.

(Not only are report programming and UI programmer very different disciplines but UI DB access and report DB access are also very different. UI access tends to jump around in the data stream, to be read / write and to require locking in order to serialize user access. Report access tends to be sequential and read-only and to involve a large number of records. This access model difference is so great that system administrators often have reports run against a read-only shadow copy of the editable database.)

In order to address the issue of report programmers needing specialized database knowledge, an IBM database expert had the idea to create a level of abstraction which would make databases easier for report writers to understand and to use. That programmer was a guy named Codd and that abstraction was the relational database, tied forever to the linguistic interface we now call SQL.

Relational Databases

The relational database model starts where the report programmer finishes: a two-dimensional data structure. This maps perfectly on to sheets of paper, or their presentation in the PDF, or their representation in HTML.

The relational model replaces record sets with "tables" and records with "row" and fields with "columns." (Note that all this replacing is at a high level of abstraction; down on the disk, it is pretty much all files, records, fields and indices.)

LINKING

The relational model does away with hard links: all linking is done via data values within indices. Imagine two tables, tblPrim and tblSec. Imagine that each these tables has a column named "user-Name." You can link the two tables on this column, like this:

```
SELECT * FROM tblPprim JOIN tblSec USING(userName);
```

If there is no index which covers userName on either table, then the "join" operation requires the DBMS to scan each row of each table to find the matches. This is certainly possible but it is slow because there is lots of work that goes on behind the scenes.

INDICES ON TABLES

An index maps a key value or values to a row. The key values are specified by a list of one or column names. An index on a single column is a "simple key." An index on multiple columns is a "complex key."

Indices come in two varieties:

• Unique which means exactly what you think it does: that every key value is unique.

• Duplicates allowed, called simply an "index," which is an index which allows duplicate key values.

PRIMARY KEY, PRIMARY INDEX

Every table has a primary index, which is the default way the DBMS will access the table. The primary index is on a primary key; usually the primary key is a simple key, but not always (we cover this under "Constraints" below).

LINKING TABLES

Let us return to our linked tables example, above. If you add an index on each of tblPrim and tblSec on userName, then the DBMS can use a "look up" function on each of the indices to find the matches.

CONSTRAINTS

"Constraints" in this context refers to rules which help the DBMS keep the data in the database correct and help the DBMS interpret queries.

Indices are very similar to constraints, in syntax and in action.

There are five kinds of constraints:

1. NOT NULL constraints which apply to individual columns; the DBMS will not set such a column to NULL.

2. UNIQUE constraints which apply to a field or set of fields; the DBMS enforces this.

3. PRIMARY KEY constraints which apply to the primary key.

4. TABLE CHECK constraints which apply to various columns in every row in a given table; the DBMS keeps a table in order.

5. FOREIGN KEY constraints (also known as Referential Integrity checks) help keep the relationships between tables

intact.

6.   INFORMATIONAL constraints are suggests about how best to access data; unlike the other constraints, the DBMS does not enforce these constraints. Instead, these constraints are used to help the DBMS retrieve and store data efficiently.

The cool part is that the DBMS can make sure that the data in the database meets some minimum standards, even if the UI or loader does not address these issues.

In a relational context, given that the links are all soft, the correctness of the data is even more critical than in other contexts.

FIRM LINKS

The relational model has a mechanism that is more than a soft link but not fully a hard link, which I call a "firm" link.

Using the RDBMS concept of the "autoincrement" data type, you can have a row ID for every table which is maintained automatically. The row ID is a simple integer which is overhead and not data, so users need never see (let alone modify) this column. In this scenario, each row has a unique, independent and unchanging ID. This row ID can be used as a primary key, to ensure the updates are handled correctly as those updates can be applied to the never-changing ID.

Transactional SQL

Transactional SQL is just what is sounds like: a dialect of SQL that has a few added feature to define transaction sets. We assume that the corresponding DBMS has support for these features, making writing applications easy and quick and making using those applications easy and safe.

Specifically, SQL has a "commit" command which means "move this transaction set from the temporary database to the production database" and a "rollback" command which means "do not apply these transactions to the production database."

Embedded versus Interactive

In case you run across these terms, we are going to consider "embedded SQL" and "interactive SQL."

Embedded SQL is SQL you find in source code, to be passed to the RDBMS for execution. It is common to see SQL statements just hanging out in the source code of almost any current programming language. This was Codd's bold vision: to wrap the interaction with the database in a linguistic interface which was constant across programming languages. This means that the database administrator does not have to know Java, or Python, or Ruby, or any other particular language: she can give you the query you need in SQL without regard to the host language. It is all SQL to her.

However, she might not be a programmer at all. She might not be writing apps to test her SQL statements. It is far more likely that she is using an interactive SQL environment, such as SQL Studio from Microsoft, or phpMyAdmin for MySQL. These environments allow her to enter an SQL statement into an application which is connected directly to the RDBMS. She can interact with the database directly which lets her perform her database administration duties without having to learn a programming environment. She can also try out the SQL statements she gives you before giving them to you. A decent interactive environment will even do some basic analysis for her: which indices were used to execute the statement, how much system time was required, etc. This feedback allows her to "tune" the schema to better support the demands placed on it by application software.

Delve Deeper, Chapter 8

1. Look up Indexed Sequential Access Method (ISAM)

2. Look up the Dewey Decimal System: how is this an example of complex keys? Of foreign keys? Of how to build and use an index?

3. Who was Codd? Why did his abstraction take over the database world so well and for so long? Why were his rules so well-chosen?

4. If your SQL schema does not use row IDs, how can you apply a change to a primary key value?

5. Google "OLTP" for historical context.

Searching & Sorting

This chapter is about the science of searching and sorting. This is something that we all think we know but so few of us study.

Knuth

Whenever we think about searching and sorting, we should think of the great Donald Knuth, a pioneer in Computer Science. His career has spanned both theory and practice, hardware and software, the abstract and the concrete.

He wrote an amazing multi-volume textbook on almost all things CS which is called "The Art of Computer Programming." Just the title gives you an idea of what Knuth was trying to do: to move programming beyond a code-slinging exercise into a fully-fledged academic subject.

(There is nothing wrong with code-slinging: we need people to write code. But brick-laying is not all there is to putting up buildings and slinging code is not all there is to building software. If you are a code slinger, then sling that code with pride and precision. But don't forget about software engineering, or design or debugging or any of the other aspects of the Art of Computer Programming.)

Knuth's "The Art of Computer Programming" is a classic and a rare book that you can skim and review and turn to when things get sticky. Some day you might want to take the time to read through the entire set, but you do not have to wait for distant day. You can get some benefit from this book right now, as much of it is on-line and many libraries have a copy (especially college libraries).

One of those chapters is called "Searching and Sorting" and it is well worth the read, but in this chapter I will give an overview so that you can make sensible choices when you have to search and sort.

Needles and Haystacks

When trying to indicate that finding something will be difficult, there is a figure of speech that you are "looking for a needle in a haystack."

Early computer scientists decided to co-opt this saying when they came up with jargon to describe searching and sorting in academic term: what you are trying to find is called "the needle" and the data set in which you are searching for the needle is called "the haystack."

Specifically, software searching for a "needle" in a "haystack" breaks down like this:

1. Identify an attribute or attributes of the needle to match.

2. Specify how to "scan" the haystack, that is how to examine each of the elements in the haystack, in whatever order is natural to the haystack or contrived by your code.

3. Test each element against the needle for a match, which means having an explicit method of comparing the needle against the current element.

4. Specify how to know that your search is done: either via the match if you find one, or the end of the list if there isn't one (sorting introduces another way out as you will see).

The Haystack

It is not surprising that the attributes of the haystack should determine how you search it and whether or not it makes sense to sort it.

The most relevent attributes are these:

1. Size: the number of elements in the data set.

2. Attributes: the elements have attributes along which they can be searched or sorted.

3.   Randomness: randomness ranges from lots (the elements are in a very random order at least according to some element).

Sorting

Sorting is relatively expensive in computer terms: it often takes both CPU time and RAM and sometimes lots of disk space.

Sorting can be done either when the data set is completed or as the data set is built. Either way it is a burden and has overhead. So when is sorting worth all this effort and overhead?

• As programmers writing code which scans a data set, we almost always access the data in some sorted order and it makes sense to keep the data in sorted order rather than sort it every time we access it.

• Sometimes the data set is so big that finding needles in it would be too slow without the advantages that sorting confers.

• Sometimes our access patterns are erratic and we need to use the speed that ISAM and other indices provide as we jump around the data.

HOW TO SORT

The attributes which affect searching also affect sorting. Just as there are many ways to search a haystack there are many says to sort a haystack. Just as we present searching with a simple version and a more sophisticated algorithm.

The simplest way to sort a data set is to scan that data set and identify the lowest value in each pass and you build a new data set in ascending order. This method is easy to code and slow to run. Is that a good trade-off? That depends on your particular situation.

A more sophisticated way to sort haystacks is called "bubble sort" because it "bubbles up" the low values to the top of the list and has the high values fall to the bottom of the list. There is a quite good article in Wikipedia on bubble sort you should read:

```
https://en.wikipedia.org/wiki/Bubble_sort
```

Simple Search

The most basic search is the most obvious: you start with the first element in the data set and test each element until you find the one you want.

For example, you can easily find a book in a single shelf by running your eye across the spines of the books until you find the one you want, even if the books are in apparently random order. This works because there are so few books to search.

In this example, the following correspondences apply:

1. The book title is the attribute that stands for the whole, the searchable attribute.

2. The book is the needle.

3. The book shelf is the haystack.

How Sorting Helps

If the haystack is sorted, then you know when you are done:

• If the needle is lower than the current element, you go on.

• If the needle matches the current element, you have found your target and you are done.

• If the needle is higher than the current element, you are done because you are sure that the needle is not in the haystack.

If the haystack is sorted, you have ways to jump into the haystack at logical points. we call these ways to jump into the haystack "indices."

Binary Search

There are many sophisticated searching techniques and algorithms but I will only consider one as an example: the binary search. If you like this kind of thing, you should find Knuth's "Searching and Sorting" chapter on line for more and better examples:

```
http://www6.uniovi.es/cscene/topics/algo/cs9-03.xml.html
```

Binary search is delightfully simple and frequently useful when searching a sorted haystack. Binary search is an example of the "divide and conquer" strategy.

1.   Divide the number of elements in the haystack in half.

2.   Jump to the middle element.

3.   Test the middle element: is it higher, lower or equal to the needled?

4.   If it is higher, you are interested in the higher half of the haystack.

5.   If it is lower, you are interested in the lower half of the haystack.

6.   If it is equal, you have found the target.

7.   Take the interesting half and repeat: jump to its middle and test.

BINARY SEARCH EXAMPLE

To illustrate this algorithm (there are many quite good examples on-line, so if this does not work for you, then you can find another) We will work through an example

Our needle is the number 70 and the haystack is a list of 20 random small integers in the range of 1 to 100 which are sorted and stored in an array with indices 0 through 19.

```
Needle: 70

Haystack:
    0     1     2     3     4     5     6     7     8     9
  +----+----+----+----+----+----+----+----+----+----+
  |  1 | 10 | 13 | 14 | 17 | 25 | 30 | 31 | 32 | 44 |
  +----+----+----+----+----+----+----+----+----+----+
  | 50 | 53 | 59 | 62 | 63 | 65 | 70 | 72 | 83 | 97 |
  +----+----+----+----+----+----+----+----+----+----+
   10    11    12    13    14    15    16    17    18    19
```

We divide the array into two halves, 0 through 9 as the lower half and 10 through 19 as the upper half. We are looking for the needle 70. We see the first item in the lower half is "50" which is lower than our needle, so the answer (if present) is in the second half.

After round one, our haystack is reduced by half: we now have only the lower half to search.

```
Needle: 70

Haystack:
   10    11    12    13    14    15    16    17    18    19
  +----+----+----+----+----+----+----+----+----+----+
  | 50 | 53 | 59 | 62 | 63 | 65 | 70 | 72 | 83 | 97 |
  +----+----+----+----+----+----+----+----+----+----+
                           ^

                        midpoint
```

The midpoint value is 63, which is lower than our needle, so our needle (if present) is in the second half.

After round two, our outgoing haystack for the next round is the second half of the incoming haystack.

```
Needle: 70

Haystack:
```

```
  15    16    17    18    19
+----+----+----+----+----+
| 65 | 70 | 72 | 83 | 97 |
+----+----+----+----+----+
          ^
          midpoint
```

The midpoint value is 73, which is higher than our needle, so needle (if present) is in the frst half.

After round three, the outgoing haystack is the first half of the incoming haystack.

```
Needle: 70

Haystack:
  15    16
+----+----+
| 65 | 70 |
+----+----+
  ^
midpoint
```

When we get down to just two elements there is no midpoint so we must arbitrarily choose one element. We pick the first one, which is lower than our needle, so the we have to check the last element and find a match.

Code Example

Let us work through a simple example in code: let us consider all the letters (only uppercase) and search them first in random order with simple search and then in sorted order with binary search:

(Note that I stole a Unix convention in my output: "min/max/avg" which stands for "minimum," "maximum" and "average." So in the first case, "1/7/4.37" means that the shortest search was 1 second, the longest search was 7 seconds and the average search was 4.73 seconds.)

```
      Sorted Haystack: ABCDEFGHIJKLMNOPQRSTUVWXYZ
Sorted, binary search: 1/7/4.73 min/max/avg

    Unsorted Haystack: DPLHNQAVEJXFUTSYWRGCOIKZMB
Unsorted, simple search: 1/26/13.50 min/max/avg
```

When we assess the performance of implementations, the trio of minimum cost, maximum cost and average cost is useful. In this case I am counting the cost as the number of iterations through the search loop.

This is useful because when we talk about performance we have to decide if we are most interested in the best case (minimum cost), the worst case (maximum cost) or the average case (average cost). In some scenarios we want to make sure that the performance is no worse than some worst case: worst case optimization. In some scenarios we want the best case to be as good as possible: best case optimizations. In some scenarios we want the usual case to be as good as possible: this is average case optimization.

The good news is that binary search, in generally, greatly outperformed simple search. The worst case of binary search versus simple search is 7 versus 26, a huge win for binary search. The best case is 1 versus 1, which is a wash: no matter how you search, sometimes you will want the first element you encounter. The average case is 4.73 versus 13.5 which is another big win for binary search.

The bad news is that the binary search was much harder to code and debug. Binary search depends on the haystack being sorted.

The code which generated this output is listed in Appendix G.

Conclusion

Alas, there is no overall best way to search all haystacks. Luckily there are generally only three criteria by which searching is judged:

• Does your search return the correct result or results?

• Does your search perform quickly enough for your users?

• Does your search put an acceptable load on the host computer?

In practice, this is how most good programmers I know approach searching:

1. Use whatever searching method is most familiar or more obvious

2. If the performance is not good enough, then review the nature of the haystack and either tweak the searching code or choose another searching algorithm.

3. If the performance is still not good enough, consider using a library function or third party searching tool.

Delve Deeper, Chapter 9

1. Scan Donald Knuth's Wikipedia entry and feel humbled by a level of accomplishment few of us can claim.

2. How would you measure the randomness of a haystack?

3. Look up "quick sort"

Networking

This chapter is about how networking is structured, how it was intended to be used and how it actually ends up being used.

Layered Architecture of Networks

This is the bare minimum you need to connect two computers together into a physical network:

1. Transport layer: it actually carries data from one place to another.

2. Network interface: it physically connects your computer device to the transport layer.

3. Network protocol: it allows the sending and receiving computers to make sense of the data they receive through the network interface.

Transport Layer

Something has to actually physically transport the data from one place to another, even if that physical transportation is via invisible radio waves moving through the air. Never forget that radio waves are invisible but not immaterial: they are not magic. They are physical, if you forget them you will be constantly puzzled by their inability to penetrate many solid objects.

Typically, the transport layer uses either copper wire cables or "wireless" (radio signals moving through the air), or both. Since networks can have many segments, some of them can be wireless while others are wired. I prefer "wired" versus "wireless" but many people use "wifi" instead of "wireless."

Most transport layers are message-oriented which means that they gather data up into chunks and send the chunks along as a unit. If you ever see a parameter called "Maximum Transfer Unit" or "MTU" on a configuration screen somewhere, this is the size of that chunk. Do not change the MTU unless you *really* know what you are doing.

Network Interface

The network interface is usually called a "NIC" (Network Interface Card) in the PC context, or "wireless NIC" if the network is wireless.

The NIC has to match the transport layer, obviously. If you have a wireless network, then you need a wireless NIC to interface to it. If you have a wired network, you need a NIC (and a cable) to interface to it.

Each NIC has a unique identifer called "a MAC address." This ID is supposed to be unique in all the world, so that even if all the world's network-capable devices were simultaneously connected and powered up, no two nodes would have the same transport layer address.

Network Protocol: IP

Once we started connecting computers together, we started needing a common language in which to exchange data and a common set of rules to govern the conversation. In order words, a network protocol specifies how a good citizen computer behaves as a network node.

It has been a long time since I have seen any networking protocol in use other than the Internet Protocol (IP) so I will assume that all networks are IP networks.

IP was created to make the Internet possible. But it is also useful for allowing your PC printer on a shared printer and for supporting your smart phone accessing a search engine from your car as you speed down the highway. IP supports all these different situations, each with different transport layers, because IP does not require or exclude any particular transport layer.

IP ADDRESSES

In the same way that the layer below has the MAC address to uniquely identify each NIC, so IP has the IP address to uniquely identify each computer. However, the transport layer's MAC address tells us very little about the network node while the IP address tells us much about the node's presence on the network or subnet (see below)

IP addresses are made of four "octets" [1] which are commonly written in "dot notation" like this:

```
192.168.1.5
```

• The first octet is 192

• The second octet is 168

• The third octet is 1

• The fourth octet is 5

The first and second octet together form a "network." In this case, 192.168 define the network.

The third octet is the "subnet" within that network. So 192.168.1 is the subnet.

The fourth octet is the node within this subnet, which gives this particular node 192.168.1.5 as its IP address.

Being nodes in the same network is like living in the same town: you can get from one to another but you need to use the roads to do it.

Being nodes in the same subnet is like having houses on the same cul-de-sac. Even if you are not right next to each other, you can get from one house to another without having to drive or having to know the layout of the town.

So 192.168.1.12 can "see" 192.168.1.5 without any kind of route or any kind of networking help. These nodes can "find" each other with the computer equivalent of sticking their heads out a window and shouting. This kind of networking is gloriously simple to set up and delightfully reliable. This is the most basic kind of Local Area Network (LAN) and if that is all you need, you are in luck: the abstraction is nearly perfect. Just plug it all in and go.

PACKET-BASED

IP is packet-based, which means that the protocol gathers up data into messages which it calls packets. Much as the layer below transfers in chunks, so this layer transmits in packets.

But unlike the layer below, packets have headers and structure which allow for much more sophisticated processing than the lower level chunks.

Transferring in packets allows every node on the network to handle the data properly. Every node can tell which packets are for that node, based on IP address.

Packets are also why IP-based LANs work so well. Imagine that the network is a set of tubes connecting all the computers. Imagine that the packets are marbles which flow around the network. Imagine that every node has a unique color: one is black, one is red and one is white. Every node sees every marble, but does not need to examine the marbles in order to function: the black node picks out the black marbles and lets the rest go by. The white node picks out the white marbles and so on. [2]

In reality, there are no tubes and no marbles but the concept is the same: each NIC reads every packet in the transport layer but each NIC knows which packets are directed at it and only passes those packets up the chain to the host computer. So each host only "sees" packets meant for it.

LAN vs WAN vs WLAN

Networks come in two basic types: local and not-local which we call "local" and "wide area."

• Local Area Networks (LANs): at the transport level this means physically connected to the same network segment; at the IP level this means on the same subnet.

• Wide Area Networks (WANs): at the transport level this means a network of networks which allow two physically separate LANs to communicate; at the IP level this means having routing in place to guide packets on the "hops" needed to get from one subnet to the other.

Sometimes it matters that a LAN or LAN segment is wireless, so we needed a way to talk about that, so this scheme was extended slightly:

• Wireless LANs (WLANs): at the transport level WLAN refers to all the authorized devices with wireless NICs in range of a given wireless access point ("wifi hot spot").

Directing Traffic

In theory, it should not matter if your device is on a LAN and you need that device to access another device on another LAN: that kind of "routing" is available from hardware for the transport layer and is built into IP. But in real life this "network topology" matters more often than you might think.

In order to make two LANs into a single LAN, which creates a *single* LAN at IP-level LAN, you need a device called "a bridge" which copies packets across the networks so the two LANs are fused into one LAN and every node on either network has access to all the nodes on both networks.

In order to get packets from one subnet to another subnet, which creates an IP-level WAN, you need a device called "a router" which knows the path from one subnet to another. The path consists of the IP address of a "gateway" which is how packets get off the LAN to the WAN.

There is an additional wrinkle: in order to make network administration easier, the good folks who defined IP set aside some networks as "private" which means that, by convention, routers are not
supposed to route packets to the WAN from them. Thus network
architects who use private networks for LANs should be reason-
ably assured that their private data will not go over the Internet.
This topic will come up in much greater detail in the chapter on
Security.

Don't worry if this story does not really make sense to you in the
abstract: much of networking becomes much clearer in context. I
will use a previous example as context at the end of this chapter.

Assigning IP Addresses

When IP was defined, there were only servers and not many of
them. Furthermore, there really were only local (same subnet)
servers and remote (over the WAN) servers.

Static IP Addresses

With only a few computers to which to assign IP addresses, and
servers to boot, it was easy enough to manually assign what are
now called "static IP addresses." Servers tend to run all the time
and to be replaced only rarely. Furthermore, even if the hardware is
replaced, there is good reason to keep the IP address the same so
that all the clients can still avail themselves of whatever service or
services the server provides.

Dynamic IP Addresses: DHCP

When the revolution of client computing arrived, suddenly there
was a huge increase in the number of addresses needed and these
addresses were not needed all the time or even to be consistent
over time, since clients need to find servers but servers merely need
to respond to clients at whatever IP address the client used. At first,

system administrators tried to manually assign IP addresses to all the client computers. This worked poorly for two reasons:

1. Since octets can only represent 0 through 255, there is a theoretical limit of 256 values for a subnet. In practice, 255 is the broadcast address so bad things will happen if you assign 255 to a network node; 0 is only valid in some IP addressing schemes. Therefore, to be safe, any subnet can only have 254 nodes within it. And you get to 254 nodes much faster than you might think.

2. Since client computers tend to be shut off much of the time, and sometimes taken out of service without telling any sysadmins, sysadmins found that their precious IP addresses were assigned to computers which didn't need them at the moment (shut off) or ever again (decommissioned).

A solution to this problem of client IP addresses was provided by one of the companies most responsible for the proliferation of client machines (desktop PCs): Microsoft. The solution was the Dynamic Host Configuration Protocol (DHCP). DHCP allows a client computer to request an IP address--remember that NICs have a MAC address, so NICs can send and receive data over a network without an IP address. The client requests an IP address from a DHCP server, which gives sys admins a measure of control. Each address assignment comes with a "lease" which expires if not renewed. So when a client computer is put into a closet, or given away, the lease expires and the address is returned to the pool.

This is another abstraction which is terrific unless and until it fails: you turn on a computer device, it configures itself as a client and then it all just works. What if your computer device does not become properly configured? There is very little that a layperson can do to debug that problem.

Worse, these days clients sometimes act as servers to other clients, so if an IP address changes at the whim of the DHCP server, the app which depends on a particular IP address will suddenly stop working.

Dynamic Name Service (DNS)

By now you have noticed that while I claim that the Internet is built on top of IP, you can type "www.ibm.com" into a browser instead of an IP address. You can type name@domain.com as an email address. This is because someone invented Domain Name Server (DNS).

The short version is that DNS takes in names and gives back IP addresses.

The long version is that DNS is a protocol supported by a network of servers around the world. This protocol accepts a domain name as input, parses that domain name and then searches the DNS registry to see if there is a corresponding IP address.

(You will notice some basic similarities to the IP notation.)

Let us consider this example, which has the optional subdomain:

```
Sub.MyDomain.com
```

Parsing the domain goes like this:

1. Break into parts using the dots: Sub, MyDomain and com.

2. Reverse the order of the parts: com, MyDomain and Sub.

3. The first part is the Top Level Domain (TLD), in our case 'com'. [3]

4. The rest of the parts are like a directory path which, when followed, arrive at an IP host on the Internet.

This allows use to have email addresses and host names which are easier to remember than IP addresses.

Video Call Example Revisited

Now we have the tools to revisit the example in the chapter entitled *Sympathy For Tech Support*. As you may remember, my wife was trying to debug the sudden failure of a teleconferencing app with the following architecture:

1. An iPad client which provides the user interface

2. A Mac Mini server which provides the actual video call

3. The client and server communicate over a WLAN

4. The server connects to other servers over the WAN

The problem seemed to be between the client and server because the server could be used to make video calls on its own.

We can revisit this example now that we know a bit about networking:

-   The client and the server have to be on the same subnet so the client can find the server. I used my iPhone to confirm that the iPad and the Mac Mini were both on the WLAN (they were).

-   The server has to have a route to the WAN so that it can send and receive data across the Internet to make the video call work. I confirmed this by bringing up a public web site on the browser.

-   The WLAN connects to the router which connects to the Internet. This must be working if the public web site comes up.

-   I used a network protocol analyzer to show that the client was not getting a response from the server. My Protocol Analyzer is a laptop running the software called Wire Shark.

-   I drafted a bug report with as much detail as was relevant and sent it off to Tech Support.

The Cloud and the Network

The Computer Cloud receives its input from the network and sends that output over the network. This means that the Cloud's public face is the network. Even though the heavy lifting is done by computers on the network, without the network there is no Cloud.

Delve Deeper, Chapter 10

1. Look up ARCNET and give a silent prayer of thanks for the current state of networking and inter-networking. Also know that my brother-in-law made an ARCNET link with a loop of wire and a water-filled styrofoam coffee cup and that as cool as it was bizarre.

Chapter 10 End Notes

[1] Octets, being groups of eight binary digits, can only represent the values from 0 through 255.

[2] I stole this excellent analogy from a TV show I saw decades ago. I have tried and failed to find the original source to credit them. I wish I could recall the source; the visual aid was so good that I still remember it all these years later.

[3] https://en.wikipedia.org/wiki/Top-level_domain

Client/Server

This chapter is about client/server architectures.

You probably already have a pretty good idea of what they are and how they work, but we want to think a bit about them formally.

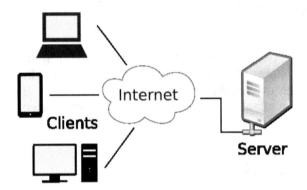

The Client/Server Model [1]

In the Client/Server model, the client makes a request and the Server satisfies that request with a response. The request is usually a message and the response is usually also a message. Messages are usually chunks of plaintext which are sent and received via a communications channel; these days almost always a TCP/IP network connection.

Common Client/Server Systems

You probably already have used many software systems which are client/server:

- Web servers serve up web pages to clients (browsers) using HTTP or HTTPS.

- Database servers serve up data to clients using any of a number of protocols to transport SQL requests from the clients to the servers and then carry back data responses from the server to the client.

- Print servers accept print requests from client machines and execute them.

- File servers accept requests to store or retrieve files from client machines.

Why Client/Server?

Before we consider a running program which uses the client/server model, let us consider what problem or problems are solved by this model.

1. Design: Client/Server creates a bright, clean line between the two parts of the system.

2. Coding: Client/Server allows the code great flexibility on their side of that bright line and options with which to test.

3. Debugging: Client/Server makes the communication between the Client and the Server explicit, which means that you can intercept or examine the communications to help debug either part.

4. System Administration: Client/Server allows the system administrator to run the Client and the Server on different machines.

5. Run-time: Client/Server allows the run-time environment to have a single image or a small number of images of the Server with which multiple Client can communicate.

Running Program (Client/Server)

Let us return to our usual starting point, a running program. In fact, I will consider two scenarios: a single running program from those dark pre-Client/Server times and a Client/Server pair.

Example App

For our example let us consider the case of a report program which runs through a database and produces a report. In either scenario, the database is governed by a DBMS.

Single Program

The report program is linked to a library which has the DBMS API. The report calls the library routines to get the data. The calls are simply function calls from one part of a program to another.

The library routines have to handle all things that a DBMS has to do: buffering, cache'ing, serializing access (handling multiple users). Each and every program on the computer system that accesses the database uses the same routines and those routines have to figure out how to keep from stepping on each other's toes.

The library routines also have to let the files system's buffering because it is very hard for different copies of the same library routines to share buffered data across different instances.

Then the report program analyzes the data to make the report, hoping that nothing that the library routines are doing causes a problem.

Client/Server Pair

The report is a program which makes a request of the server. The server might be on the same computer, but might be on another computer. The server processes the request and provides a response. The report processes the response and creates the report.

Note how much simpler and shorter this scenario is and how much less the report program has to do. This is part of the glory of Client/Server: a division of labor which keeps the complexity in the server but the server has only one job, so the complexity is mitigated.

The Client/Server architecture spread like wildfire because it dovetails so nicely with the Internet, with the World Wide Web, with TCP/IP and interactions which cross organizational boundaries. The client can run inside your office, your department, your company while the server runs in the same office (LAN) or in the IT department (VLAN) or from how to the IT department (WAN) at a trusted external site (VPN).

Delve Deeper, Chapter 11

1. Look up Indexed Sequential Access Method (ISAM)

2. When it comes to handling multiple users accessing the same resource, check out the mutex and the semaphore; for extra credit, compare and contrast them. Or let the Internet do that for you.

3. Compare LAN, VLAN, VPN and WAN

Chapter 11 End Notes

1   https://upload.wikimedia.org/wikipedia/commons/thumb/c/c9/Client-server-model.svg/500px-Client-server-model.svg.png

Debugging

This chapter is about how to approach debugging technology in a rigorous, orderly fashion, using the tools we have covered in this book so far.

Debugging Overview

In concept, debugging is deceptively simple:

1. Get a bug report which defines the bad behavior and, God willing, the input which triggers that bad behavior.

2. Match that bad behavior up with the code that generated that bad behavior, using any of the three kinds of debugging.

3. Fix that bad behavior by modifying the code.

4. Confirm that the fix not only fixes the problem but does not cause any new problems. Don't forget this step. Don't skip this step. Don't leave this step for when you have more time.

Of course this is a gross simplification but it is useful to always remember that you need all these steps and you cannot skip them or shuffle them. You need to know what is wrong. You need to know how it went wrong. You need to know how to fix it. You need to know that you have succeeded and so are done.

STAKEHOLDERS

Now it is time to reveal one of debugging's darkest secrets: it begins and ends with the stakeholder, the person or persons who reported the issue and the person or persons who certify that you have fixed it.

If you take up programming as a hobby or self-taught, you are the stakeholder. This is a pretty sweet deal: you decide what needs to be done, how it should be done, which issues are worth fixing and which are not.

The moment you have teachers, or users, or teammates, or colleagues, or employers, you are no longer the stakeholder. This is an adjustment and this adjustment is sometimes painful. However there are benefits to having stakeholders: they often see things we cannot see and they often do not share our blind spots. They can push us to be better.

Too many programmers feel that they are the final authority with regard to their software even after stakeholders arrive on the scene.

Do the right thing. Start with the stakeholder to figure out what is wrong. Finish with the stakeholder to confirm that you are done.

Baked In

There are two properties which really should be "baked into" software, ideally at the design stage but certainly from the beginning of the implementation stage: security and "debugability" (ease of debugging).

Security is a topic in its own right and will be considered in depth another time, but security (or lack of it) is so deep in computer that is not the last appearance "security" will make in this chapter. For now, it is enough to say that security features often make debugging harder and debugging features often compromise security.

Ease of debugging is rarely the design or implementation priority that they should be. This is a shame because trying to retrofit software to be easy to debug after it has been written is pretty difficult.

Before we discuss how to build in ease of debugging we need to define debugging.

The Theoretical Part

Debugging is about finding and removing bugs. Bugs are unexpected or unacceptable output for legal input. This assumes that you know what is supposed to happen and that you know what actually happened. This assumes that you know both the input and the output. In other words, that you have a valid bug report. Ah, bug reports, how you vary in quality and clarity. How you vary so much in both quality and clarity.

Once you have a bug report, you are ready to start finding and fixing bugs. To do that you are going to have to diagnose the problem, craft a solution, test and deploy an update.

Diagnosing bugs is the process of matching errant behavior with the code causing that errant behavior. This makes "the repeatable case" so important: if you can run the software against the problematic input or inputs, you can work on the issue in a predictable and iterative manner. If you do not have a repeatable case, your options dwindle quickly.

One skill that can is consistently undervalued in debugging is being able to shift levels of abstraction. With luck, the problem area will be obvious but all too often figuring out where to turn your attention is, itself, a big project.

Basic Types of Debugging

In my experience with debugging, there are three basic approaches: high-level, medium-level and low-level. High-level debugging is the easiest and promises to be the quickest but often is not. Medium-level debugging is a bit harder and a bit harder, but seems to be the most "natural" option. Alas, this approach simply cannot find certain kinds of bugs. Low-level debugging is the biggest commitment and has the most overhead and often seems like too much trouble, but it is the most powerful debugging tool in the debugging tool box.

High-Level

High-level debugging consists primarily of source code review and meditation. Literally. I see people pull up the source code and then frown in deep thought while they simply figure out where the problem lies and how to fix it.

This approach is fine under the following circumstances:

• the problem is trivial, a typo in output for example;

• the code is clear in your head and you are confident that you can see how the failure occurred and how to fix it;

• the problem is clear in your head, you have encountered it before or you recently found a similar bug and you are already mostly there.

Even if you are not in any of these scenarios, sometimes you have no choice: if you lack a repeatable case or your code cannot run in a test environment or the failure does not occur in the test environment then this may be your only option.

Be warned: this approach either works well or it is a time-consuming and inefficient and frustrating way to squash a bug.

Medium-Level

Medium-level debugging consists primarily of adding print statements to the code to provide feedback on the internals of the software as the software runs and fails.

For some reason, this is many programmers' first instinct. This is a perfectly adequate way to find many bugs in application code you control.

If the bug lies somewhere else, for instance in code you do not control (a library routine, a colleague's code, et cetera) then this approach is useless.

This approach has another, sometimes devastating, drawback: you are changing the software you are debugging. In most cases, you keep the changes trivial and this drawback is unlikely to bite you in the butt. But every now and then the fact that you are changing the thing you are trying to fix really bites you in the butt. It bites hard and deep. If you do not have a Plan B, you will be chasing your tail and reaching for back ups.

Low-Level

Low-level debugging consists primarily of using software at a lower level than your code. In an interpreted environment, the interpreter almost always has a debugging mode which you can use to run your code in debugging mode. In a compiled environment you can use a low-level debugger; for instance for C and C++ programs running in Unix and Unixoid environments such as Linux you can use the powerful *gdb*.

With low-level debugging, you generally have at least these features:

- memory inspection: finding out the values of variables and structures in RAM;

- break points: break points stop program execution at a particular point in the source code;

- watch points: break points tripped by specified variables having specified values;

- call stack trace: how the current execution point was reached, usually a list of function calls either from your code or from system calls;

Using these features you should be able to see what is "really" going on. To take full advantage of these features you have to understand what is going on, which is why this chapter comes so late in the book. Access to the low-level functions and memory structures will do you no good if these things mean nothing to you.

Role of Design & Implementation

Now we explore what is meant by "debugability" and "baked in" above.

If your design is clean and modular, then associating failures with the corresponding software module is easier. If your coding is clean and clear, then associating failures with the corresponding code is easier.

If your implementation has reasonable logging, debugging will be easier. Logging has to be done in moderation because disk space and CPU time are not unlimited. But a properly logged break crumb can be the difference between a quick log review and a full-blown bug hunt.

If your implementation has check points, debugging will be easier. Check points are a special kind of logging which lets the future bug hunter know these things: a system time, an application status and any other information which might help on a bug hunt. Ideally, the check point is a mark of the last time every thing was well. Check points are a great way to debug a server which runs perpetually in the background.

If your implementation has a debug mode, in which the print statements and other changes are not new, but have been "baked in" and tested and validated so switching into debug mode is less risky.

If your code is loosely organized, then tracking control-flow through it will be harder. If your code is sloppy then tracking data changes will be harder. You may discover, as so many of us have already discovered, that there is often a trade off between coding speed and maintaining pain. Code faster, debug slower, change with more pain.

Sometimes coding quickly is a requirement. Sometimes coding quickly is a habit. Sometimes coding quickly is a personality trait. Until you have taken software through its life cycle, until you have had to debug and patch and upgrade and release, you don't really know what your coding style really *means*. A big part of maturing as a coder is debugging your code and other people's code. How you code informs how you debug.

You will be amazed at how different code looks when you are trying to figure out what is going wrong. The clever code can seem opaque. The powerful code can seem baroque. The simple code can seem like a cool drink of water on a hot summer's day.

The Practical Part

In practice, programmers usually go through these approaches in that order:

1. High-level: take a shot based on your first impression, perhaps backed up with a quick code review.

2. Medium-level: if the high-level approach does not work, you take a longer look at the source code and then maybe add a print statement or two which hopefully gives you insight into the problem.

3. Low-level: if the medium-level approach does not work, you sigh deeply and perhaps even find a wizard who understands the low-level environment to help you as you wander through the weeds.

Whichever level of debugging you choose, let us quickly review the four things we have to do in order to find and fix a bug.

1. Define the problem in terms of the code

2. Associate the problem with the code

3. Solve the problem by changing the code

4. Validate the patch

THE CURIOUS CASE OF SHERLOCK HOLMES

The information gathering phase of debugging feels like detective work. I have never been a police detective, but I suspect that the similarities are pretty superficial. But that does not stop programmers from enjoying murder mysteries and using the vocabulary of fictional detectives.

When facing down a bug, we would all like to be the Sherlock Holmes of the big reveal, to pause briefly and then, through acute observation of minute detail and amazing powers of deduction, voila! The answer springs forth organically from the premises, the observations and cold, hard logic.

The problem is that all too often we are the doldrums Sherlock Holmes: confused and angry and frustrated that the pieces don't make sense. With a Sherlock Holmes mystery, we are assured that after the doldrums will come the big reveal. With a bug hunt, we are assured of very little.

Once you eliminate the impossible, whatever remains, no matter how improbable, must be the truth.

Arthur Conan Doyle's Sherlock Holmes

The difference between those two Sherlock Holmeses is the blinding flash of insight, the epiphany, the moment of clarity. All too often the stumbling block is pride and laziness and the unwillingness to eliminate only the impossible. All too often we eliminate lots of stuff, often based on guesswork and prejudice. Discipline is required to eliminate only the impossible. Whatever remains, no matter how improbable, must be the truth.

I really enjoyed reading all the Sherlock Holmes stories. I love the way everything gets wrapped up at the end. I also understand that this is an entertaining fiction and not a role model. No one but Watson likes Holmes. Or can stand to work with him.

So resist the pretty party trick of trying to pull the bug out of thin air. Do the legwork. Choose the appropriate level of debugging, but make sure that you go as low as you have to. In debugging, there is no place for hubris or vanity. Do the legwork. Find the bug. Fix the bug. Repeat as needed.

And when the script breaks down, when the bug is intractable and the situation seems impossible, remember that sometimes you need to go back to square one and need to question your assumptions. Oh, those assumptions, how we love them! How useful they are so much of the time, but how bitter is their infrequent betrayal. So many hours of time and effort have been flushed down the toilet of wrong assumptions, out-of-date assumptions, mostly-correct assumptions. When it is darkest and despair is just around the corner, remember this:

Once you eliminate the impossible, whatever remains, no matter how improbable, must be the truth.

When hunting bugs, the truth is our dearest friend.

Testing

We have covered our options for finding the bug. We glossed over the fixing part because the fixing part is really just a kind of programming and if you could write the program in the first place you should be able to code around the problem. Now it is time to talk about the end of the debugging process: testing.

You can try to skip the testing phase of debugging, but it cannot be done. If you don't test then you are leaving your users to test. There is no way out of it. The testing question reminds me of the bumper sticker:

Failing to plan is planning to fail.

Testing Overview

Testing is peculiar to each implementation and the ease of testing varies wildly from situation to situation. But in almost every case, testing is easier if testing was a design goal and an implementation goal.

Testing is when you ensure that your code matches the specification. Concretely, testing is when you run pre-determined inputs through software and confirm that the output is the expected output.

1. Input

2. Process

3.   Output

4.   Confirm

Unit Testing

Unit testing is a big topic but for our purposes, unit testing is testing which breaks up software into to separate "units" which can be tested and validated individually. In theory, unit testing is part of the development process: you should have been using unit testing as you built the software so in theory debugging should be a natural part of that process.

Regression Testing

Regression testing is a big topic but for our purposes, regression testing is running software through a test set which is intended not only to confirm that the bug has been fixed but that no new bugs were introduced in the process. Essentially, regression testing is running all the old tests in addition to the new test. Regression testing is how we have confidence that our new version is bug-free.

Delve Deeper, Chapter 12

1.   Check out **Debugging the Development Process** by Steve Maguire.

2.   Figure out what low-level debugger options you have and how to set a break point using one of those options.

3.   Review "dangling else disease"

4.   Check out "the fence post problem"

Encryption & Compression

This chapter is about data encryption and compression: these are separate but similar topics.

Note that this chapter is not a mathematical analysis but rather a high-level description of these topics to give you an introduction, a jumping off point for further study if you are so inclined.

What Is Encryption?

Encryption is a process which protects the contents of a file or files from unauthorized access. Encryption changes its input data in such a way that (in theory) can only be undone with a related process (decryption) and the key.

CRACKING

Since encryption is about stopping people from doing something, you have to assume that a bad actor will try to break or crack your encryption. Sometimes the bad actor is a maladjusted malcontent who thinks that doing something forbidden is cool (see the chapter on ethics). Sometimes the bad actor is a professional criminal who hopes to use the decrypted data to commit crimes. Sometimes, if you are really unlucky, the bad actor is a well-funded, well-trained and disciplined team of professionals who work for a foreign government. That is a grim scenario.

In fact many security professionals measure the strength of encryption by the amount of time it takes to crack it. Security professionals are comfortable assessing the likely attackers and the level of threat posed by these likely attackers.

Encryption Demo

I found a very simple example of encryption created for education-al purposes at the URL below. I tweaked the output slightly to make it prettier.

```
http://c-program-example.com/2012/04/c-program-to-encrypt-
and-decrypt-a-password.html
```

This is a "toy" implementation whose only purpose is to demon-strate a very simple encryption. Its output looks like this:

```
Enter a password: figaro
Input value     = figaro
Encrypted value = [28][31][29][23][40][37]
Decrypted value = figaro
```

Note that the encrypted value is out of the printable ASCII range, so I tweaked the code to print out the encrypted value as binary numbers. The code is provided as Appendix F.

Production Encryption

In production encryption systems, the math used to encrypt the da-ta is much more complex than the example and the key is used in a rather more integral way.

The longer the key (that is, the more bits) the larger the search space for possible keys, but the more computing power is needed to encrypt or decrypt.

Experts tend to measure the strength of encryption in terms of how long the adversary will take to crack it. But this requires a good profile of the adversary and their computing resources. Most of us are content to know that a private citizen would not be able to crack our encryption with normal (i.e. no super-computer) re-sources in a time frame to be worth it. We can assume that a non-governmental adversary will not keep at it for years.

Encryption + Compression

Production encryption usually also includes compression, for two reasons:

1. Saving disks space and / or transmission time is always a good idea

2. Compression actually enhances the encryption since lots many cracking algorithms look for patterns in the encrypted data and those patterns are obscured by compression.

What Is Compression?

Compression is a process which shrinks the contents of a file or files in such a way that the shrunken data can be returned to its original state (by decompression).

Compression can be lossless (nothing is lost in the compress / decompress process) or lossy (an acceptable amount is lost in the compress / decompress process). In most situations, "lossy" compression is unacceptable: you want all the data to come out the other end, and you want all the data to be the same. But in some applications, notable delivering images over the web, there are times when the source image's resolution far outstrips the target display device. If the display device cannot handle the resolution, why not lose it? The resolution is excess in this case and there is no point in wasting network bandwidth transmitting useless resolution. In this case, lossy compression is just what the doctor ordered.

Similarities

Encryption and compression are fundamentally similar: encryption substitutes elements in the source data with something related but hard to guess, while compression substitutes elements in the source data with something related but shorter.

In both cases, the basic algorithm is the same:

1. Take an input file to be the input data; for compression, it helps if the input data is at least a minimum size and ideally a bit repetitious.

2. Run the file's contents through a mathematical transformation: encryption uses a key to transform and compression uses a table to transform.

3. Write out the transformed data, either overwriting the original or creating a new file, depending on implementation.

Decryption and decompression are also very similar:

1. Take an input file to the input data; for compression, you want the compression algorithm to be obvious. For decryption, you might want the encryption algorithm to be obvious; you certainly want the key to be a secret.

2. Run the file's contents through the reverse mathematical transformation, which should return the input data to the original input data.

3. Write out the untransformed data, either overwriting the input or creating a new file, depending on implementation.

This is why so many compression applications offer at least weak encryption.

Compression: Huffman Coding For Example

My favourite example of compression is Huffman Coding. There is plenty of information about Huffman Coding on the web but I will go over the basics anyway.

The website GeeksForGeeks has a great quick description:

Huffman coding is a lossless data compression algorithm. The idea is to assign variable-length codes to input characters, lengths of the assigned codes are based on the frequencies of corresponding characters. The most frequent character gets the smallest code and the least frequent character gets the largest code. Huffman coding based is a delightfully simple idea: create a table of the most common letter sequences to create a table of letter sequences and then use letters.

```
www.geeksforgeeks.org/greedy-algorithms-set-3-huffman-
coding/
```

The compression process is pretty straightforward:

1. Analyze the input data to build the table

2. Read through the input data, outputting the mapped sequence if there is one; otherwise output the input data unchanged

The table maps characters to the sequences they encode. The table is to decompressing as a key to decrypting: without the table, the compressed data is very difficult to decipher. is, in some sense, a key to decrypting.

There is an implementation, in Perl, of Huffman coding and decoding which is intended for educational purposes. Since this implementation is educational, it is slanted toward ease of reading and not maximum efficiency.

I downloaded this implementation from the URL below to check it out.

```
http://www.perlmonks.org/?node_id=603111
```

As an exercise, I ran the text of the Programming Language chapter of this book through the Huffman coding and back; it worked (the output matched the input) and was pretty effective (the compressed version is only 61% as big as the original version).

File	Description	Size	Delta
prog-lang.do	Original file	40,679	
prog-lang.do.huff	Huffman code	24,925	31%

```
| prog-lang.do.unhuff | Uncompressed  | 40,679 |        |
+--------------------+---------------+--------+-------+
| prog-lang.do.gz     | GZIP version  | 15,473 |   62% |
+--------------------+---------------+--------+-------+
```

The demonstration Huffman program shrank the source data by
about a third, which is pretty good for an educational tool. For
comparison, I ran the very common gzip tool on the same data and
gzip shrank the source data by almost twice that. gzip for comparison of production version; introduce md5sum as related;

MD5SUM

This is a good time to mention MD5Sum. MD5Sum is a kind of
one-way super compression, a kind of summary so summarized
that the source data is unrecognizable. This is why MD5Sum output is called a "digest" because it is a shortened version.

The cool part is that the MD5Sum is almost certainly unique for
any given input data. This means that the MD5Sum can be used to
make sure that a given file is the version you think it is. This is why
MD5 digests was so often used with downloads so that users have
confidence about what they download.

I used the MD5Sum to confirm that the Huffman coding process's
output matched the input exactly. The MD5Sum for the input
matched the MD5Sum of the output.

ERROR CORRECTION CODES

These days the most common use for ECC I see is in high-end
RAM. Wikipedia has a rather write up of the basic concepts:

https://en.wikipedia.org/wiki/ECC_memory

COMPRESSION TRADE-OFF

The eternal trade-off of space (number of bytes) versus time (how long it takes to compress and decompress) is very true for compression. How to make the trade-off depended on the context, which was almost always either storing data on precious, expensive disk or transferring data across slow and only quasi-dependable serial communication lines.

When storing data on disk, mostly for archive purposes, we wanted minimum size and were not that concerned about how long the compression took because we were not going access the data very often or very urgently.

Back in the bad old days of sending files at 1200 baud, we were pretty excited to get the kind of 31% compression which Huffman coding afforded us. The fact that Huffman coding was quick to do and undo was a big deal.

Serial lines send data as bits. Serial lines were prone to "noise" which sometimes interfered with the signal, the good data. This meant that the occasional bit was flipped or missing. That was bad for business.

To address this issue, we used some of that precious saved space that we got from the Huffman coding to support Error detection and Correction Codes (ECC). These codes were a kind of overhead that allows us to detect errors and even correct them.

The simplest of these schemes was the *parity bit* which only detected errors and only detected a certain level of error. Essentially the parity bit was a simple binary flag added to a byte or sequence of bytes. The simplest possible parity scheme is that the parity was 1 if the number of 1's in the byte was odd and 0 if the number of 1's in the byte was even. This will allow you to perform a basic check on whether or not the byte arrived intact.

Further up the complexity chain were checksums which cost more space but did a better job detecting errors.

Error correction codes were even cooler (and took up even more space and more CPU time to process) so it was not always worth it to use them unless you knew you were using a bad line.

Encryption

All encryption is used to prevent authorized access to a given data set. When choosing an encryption scheme the first question to ask yourself is from whom is the encryption protecting the data?

Encrypting internal archives from casual viewing or accidental is one thing; trying to protect communications traffic from all comers across the wild and wooly Internet is another thing entirely.

KEYS VERSUS PRIVATE / PUBLIC KEYS

In the case where you are both the one who encrypts and the one who decrypts the data, you can use a single key and you can choose the level of encryption based on how serious you perceive the threat to be. That key has to be private because one someone has the key, they have your data. This is sometimes called "symmetric" encryption because the same key is used for both operations.

In the case where you want to send encrypted data to another party, they have to be able to decrypt it. This is usually accomplished with public key encryption, sometimes called "asymmetric" encryption.

(When encryption communications you could use a simple private key system, but then you have the dreaded "key exchange" problem: how do you secure the key when you send it? Ideally, you do the exchange through some other channel so your enemy has to compromise both channels. Sometimes we call this "out of band" by analogy with "out of band signalling.")

With public key encryption, two (mathematically compatible) keys are used: the recipient's public key to encrypt and a compatible private key to decrypt. The recipient created both keys at the same time as part of a matching pair. The public key is just that: public. The private key is a secret. This is how the process is asymmetric: one key to encrypt, another key to decrypt.

Conclusion

Compression is an essential part of current system administration, especially back up and archive.

Encryption is an essential part of current system administration, for both back up and many kinds of communications.

As a modern application programmer, you have a few obligations with regard to compression and encryption:

1. Build ease of upgrade into your app design: the one thing I can confidently predict about both compression and encryption will change dramatically and quickly as computer power grows and security issues are found and fixed.

2. Understand the time / space trade off and make good decisions for your particular situation (with an eye on item 1 above).

3. Use the strongest encryption you can, given the constraints of key distribution and CPU time.

4. Always be aware of data access issues: privacy is hard to protect and easy to lose. Err on the side of caution, but be aware of safety issues: having a backup when you need one, but not being able to access it because someone lost the key at some point, is bummer of epic proportions. Or so I hear.

Delve Deeper, Chapter 13

1. Read the Wikipedia entry on Huffman Coding

2. Look up MD5 digest or MD5 sum

3. How fast is 1200 baud? How does it compare to common data transfer speeds today?

4. What is a serial line?

5. What is a parity bit? What is a checksum? What is a Cyclic Redundancy Check?

6. How do error correction coding schemes work?

7. Why does high-end RAM (often for servers) have ECC? How often docs RAM fail, requiring ECC.

8. What is out of band signalling?

Ethics for CS

This chapter is about how to be a good citizen in the technology context. This chapter covers both how to build ethic technology and how to use technology ethically.

Glossary

Let us get some definitions out of the way:

Morals are guidelines one uses to live one's life. Everyone should have a moral code and that moral code should help one make difficult decisions. Morals are enforced by your conscience.

Ethics are the moral code which governs a particular activity. The legal profession has its own ethics. The medical profession has its own ethics. Ethics are usually enforced by professional associations but less mature professions, such as computer programming, have yet to develop a formal ethics code. That does not excuse you from behaving in an ethical manner. You know what you should do, I hope.

Laws are the rules which govern public behaviour in a society. Laws are enforced by police and courts. Staying within the bounds of law is something every citizen should be able to do.

Cyber Code of Ethics

Until we have a more formal code of ethics, I propose the following for programmers and technologists:

1. Don't break it without permission

2. Don't take it without permission

3. Don't fake it without permission

It took a while to boil precepts down into pithy, rhyming little statements. Before we get to the long versions, let us take a quick detour into the dark and dank domain of intention.

Why 'Without Permission'?

Why you do things sometimes matters. "It's the thought that counts" is one of my least favorite aphorisms because it is so often false, and all too often an excuse.

But it is true sometimes and those times are important. And in cyberspace, intention matters all the time.

Explaining intent's role is a rare case that I think that examples are more helpful than prose.

PHYSICAL LOCKS

Locksmiths and burglars have very similar skill sets but one group provides an important service and the other group are criminals who steal from other people.

BREAKING SECURITY

Much like locksmiths and burglars, system administrators help people get into ailing or locked computers while crackers try to steal data and violate privacy.

Rule 1 (Long Version)

Don't break it without permission. Consider the rather typical case of a young hacker having a go at a server on the Internet and finding a vulnerability. If you exploit that vulnerability to engage in vandalism, so you can prove that you were there, then you are behaving unethically. If you write up a quick report on the vulnerability and submit that report to whoever runs the server, then you are an aggressive jerk but you are (barely) within the bounds of ethics. (You may be out of the bounds of law however.)

Remember: just because you can do something does not mean you should do that thing. Really. And because you can do it does not make it ethical or legal or moral.

Sociologists distinguish between taboos and strictures. Taboos are rules which are enforced only by social convention. Strictures are enforced by mechanisms such as locks, or walls or cops. The problem with locks, walls, fines or cops is that they can be defeated. They can be circumvented. They can be defeated. If they are defeated, it is tempting to conclude that the ethical, legal or moral issues are also defeated. This is a kind of pragmatic morality and like so much of pragmatic morality, it is an illusion. Getting over the orchard wall does not entitle you to an apple. Getting over the orchard wall is a physical feat but the ethical, legal and moral issues remain and still demand an answer. "Why" still matters and vanity does not justify anything.

Rule 2 (Long Version)

Don't take it without permission. Just because you can access a computer resource without proper authorization does not make it ok. Just because you steal something at your keyboard does not change the stealing part. Cyber laws and cyber ethics are not very different from non-cyber ethics: stealing is wrong. Breaking other people's stuff is wrong. Imagine your actions mapped onto the non-cyber world. Walking down a street and trying every car door handle until you find an unlocked car is not acceptable. How is looking for unlocked cars different from looking for vulnerabilities on servers? Access is not granted by ineffective or outdated or inept security.

Even if this is the basis of so many heist movies (even though some of those movies are pretty good: check out the Thomas Crown Affair).

Rule 3 (Long Version)

Don't fake it without permission. Sometimes we need to satisfy old or confused or outdated software's security by faking credentials. Sometimes we need to fake out conditions which no longer apply: Virtual Machines for hardware platforms which no longer run. Sometimes we fake out conditions to make things work. None of this excuses forging credentials or forging anything else. Don't fake it without permission, even if there is a bit of rush in successfully creating a fake.

Conclusion

Determining which courses of action are ethical and which are not is generally not very difficult. Sometimes *making* the ethical choice is hard, but claiming that "because I could do it, I thought that I was allowed to do it?"

Delve Deeper, Chapter 14

1. Does your school or employer has a cyber ethics code?

2. Watch the Thomas Crown Affair

Appendix A: **Faux ASM prog1**

This is the source code for our first FASM program, "prog1."

```
; prog1 -- sample FASM program.
; executing '(4 + 9) - (10 + 2)'

; add 4 and 9, store at 0
set
1
4
set
2
9
add
stor
2
0


; subtract 10 and 2, store at 1
set
1
10
set
2
2
add
stor
2
1


; load the first partial result into 1
load
1
1
load
2
0
sub
```

This is the FASM output from assembling prog1.asm.

```
P8B (Puny 8 Bit Processor) app
P8B Assembler  in: prog1.asm
P8B Assembler out: prog1.p8b 27 bytes done.
```

This is the FASM output from executing prog1.p8b.

```
P8B (Puny 8 Bit Processor) app
P8B Emulator  in: prog1.p8b 27 bytes
[  0] Op Code: 1 (SET ) R1:   4 R2:    0
[  3] Op Code: 1 (SET ) R1:   4 R2:    9
[  6] Op Code: 5 (ADD ) R1:   4 R2:   13
[  7] Op Code: 4 (STOR) R1:   4 R2:   13
[ 10] Op Code: 1 (SET ) R1:  10 R2:   13
[ 13] Op Code: 1 (SET ) R1:  10 R2:    2
[ 16] Op Code: 5 (ADD ) R1:  10 R2:   12
[ 17] Op Code: 4 (STOR) R1:  10 R2:   12
[ 20] Op Code: 3 (LOAD) R1:  12 R2:   12
[ 23] Op Code: 3 (LOAD) R1:  12 R2:   13
[ 26] Op Code: 6 (SUB ) R1:  12 R2:    1
P8B Emulator: done at byte 27
```

This is the output of disassembling prog2.p8b.

```
P8B (Puny 8 Bit Processor) app
P8B Disassembler:  in: prog1.p8b 27 bytes
; Disassembler output
SET       ; Byte   0
   1      ; Byte   1
   4      ; Byte   2
SET       ; Byte   3
   2      ; Byte   4
   9      ; Byte   5
ADD       ; Byte   6
STOR      ; Byte   7
   2      ; Byte   8
   0      ; Byte   9
SET       ; Byte  10
   1      ; Byte  11
  10      ; Byte  12
SET       ; Byte  13
```

```
   2      ; Byte   14
   2      ; Byte   15
ADD       ; Byte   16
STOR      ; Byte   17
   2      ; Byte   18
   1      ; Byte   19
LOAD      ; Byte   20
   1      ; Byte   21
   1      ; Byte   22
LOAD      ; Byte   23
   2      ; Byte   24
   0      ; Byte   25
SUB       ; Byte   26
; eof
```

Appendix B: **Faux ASM prog2**

This is the source code for our second FASM program, "prog2."

```
; prog2 -- sample FASM program: prog1 but with variables
; evaluating '(4 + 9) - (10 + 2)'

; declare two variables, one to hold each subexpression
decl
exp1
decl
exp2

; add 4 and 9, store in exp1
set
1
4
set
2
9
add
stor
2
exp1

; subtract 10 and 2, store exp2
set
1
10
set
2
2
add
stor
2
exp2

; sub subtracts R1 from R2, so exp2 goes into R1
load
1
exp2
; sub subtracts R1 from R2, so exp1 goes into R2
load
```

```
2
exp1
sub
;
; let us try out the fancy new output instructions
;

; outn prints R2 as a number
; R2 still has the result in it
outn

; outs prints R2 as a character (text)
; set to 65 which is ASCII 'A'
set
2
65
outs
; EOF
```

This is the FASM output from assembling prog2.asm.

```
P8B (Puny 8 Bit Processor) app
P8B Assembler  in: prog2.asm
P8B Assembler out: prog2.p8b 32 bytes done.
```

This is the FASM output from executing prog2.p8b.

```
P8B (Puny 8 Bit Processor) app
P8B Assembler  in: prog2.asm
P8B Assembler out: prog2.p8b 32 bytes done.
P8B (Puny 8 Bit Processor) app
P8B Emulator  in: prog2.p8b 32 bytes
[  0] Op Code: 1 (SET ) R1:   4 R2:   0
[  3] Op Code: 1 (SET ) R1:   4 R2:   9
[  6] Op Code: 5 (ADD ) R1:   4 R2:  13
[  7] Op Code: 4 (STOR) R1:   4 R2:  13
[ 10] Op Code: 1 (SET ) R1:  10 R2:  13
[ 13] Op Code: 1 (SET ) R1:  10 R2:   2
[ 16] Op Code: 5 (ADD ) R1:  10 R2:  12
[ 17] Op Code: 4 (STOR) R1:  10 R2:  12
[ 20] Op Code: 3 (LOAD) R1:  12 R2:  12
[ 23] Op Code: 3 (LOAD) R1:  12 R2:  13
```

```
[ 26] Op Code: 6 (SUB ) R1:  12 R2:    1
[ 27] Op Code: 7 (OUTN) R1:  12 R2:    1
OUTPUT> 1
[ 28] Op Code: 1 (SET ) R1:  12 R2:   65
[ 31] Op Code: 8 (OUTS) R1:  12 R2:   65
OUTPUT> A
P8B Emulator: done at byte 32
```

This is the output of disassembling prog2.p8b.

```
P8B (Puny 8 Bit Processor) app
P8B Disassembler:  in: prog2.p8b 32 bytes

; Disassembler output
SET       ; Byte   0
  1       ; Byte   1
  4       ; Byte   2
SET       ; Byte   3
  2       ; Byte   4
  9       ; Byte   5
ADD       ; Byte   6
STOR      ; Byte   7
  2       ; Byte   8
  0       ; Byte   9
SET       ; Byte  10
  1       ; Byte  11
 10       ; Byte  12
SET       ; Byte  13
  2       ; Byte  14
  2       ; Byte  15
ADD       ; Byte  16
STOR      ; Byte  17
  2       ; Byte  18
  1       ; Byte  19
LOAD      ; Byte  20
  1       ; Byte  21
  1       ; Byte  22
LOAD      ; Byte  23
  2       ; Byte  24
  0       ; Byte  25
SUB       ; Byte  26
OUTN      ; Byte  27
SET       ; Byte  28
```

```
    2      ; Byte  29
   65      ; Byte  30
OUTS       ; Byte  31
; eof
```

Appendix C: **Faux ASM prog3**

This is the source code for our third FASM program, "prog3."

Note that there is no fancy whitespace in this version; since FASM assembler has the property that every line generates a byte, leaving out blank lines means that the output byte offset is the same as line number - 1 (because the byte offsets are zero-based ane lines are generally numbered from one). That makes figuring out the target PC for BRNE or JMP is way easier.

```
set                 ; set
1                   ; register 1
4                   ; value of 4
set                 ; set
2                   ; register 2
5                   ; value of 5
brne                ; branch not equal
14                  ; byte to jump to
set                 ; set
2                   ; register 2
78                  ; value 'N'
outs                ; output a string
jmp                 ; the else
18                  ;
set                 ; set
2                   ; register 2
89                  ; value 'Y'
outs                ; output a string
set                 ; set
2                   ; register 2
1                   ; value of 1
outn                ; output a number
```

This is the FASM output from assembling prog3.asm.

```
P8B (Puny 8 Bit Processor) app
P8B Assembler  in: prog3.asm
P8B Assembler out: prog3.p8b 22 bytes done.
```

This is the FASM output from executing prog3.p8b.

```
P8B (Puny 8 Bit Processor) app
P8B Emulator  in: prog3.p8b 22 bytes
[  0] Op Code:  1 (SET ) R1:    4 R2:    0
[  3] Op Code:  1 (SET ) R1:    4 R2:    5
[  6] Op Code: 10 (BRNE) R1:    4 R2:    5
[  8] Op Code:  1 (SET ) R1:    4 R2:   78
[ 11] Op Code:  8 (OUTS) R1:    4 R2:   78
OUTPUT> N
[ 12] Op Code: 11 (JMP ) R1:    4 R2:   78
[ 18] Op Code:  1 (SET ) R1:    4 R2:    1
[ 21] Op Code:  7 (OUTN) R1:    4 R2:    1
OUTPUT> 1
P8B Emulator: done at byte 22
```

This is the output of disassembling prog3.p8b.

```
; Disassembler output
SET       ; Byte    0
   1      ; Byte    1
   4      ; Byte    2
SET       ; Byte    3
   2      ; Byte    4
   5      ; Byte    5
BRNE      ; Byte    6
  14      ; Byte    7
SET       ; Byte    8
   2      ; Byte    9
  78      ; Byte   10
OUTS      ; Byte   11
JMP       ; Byte   12
  18      ; Byte   13
SET       ; Byte   14
   2      ; Byte   15
  89      ; Byte   16
OUTS      ; Byte   17
SET       ; Byte   18
   2      ; Byte   19
   1      ; Byte   20
OUTN      ; Byte   21
```

Appendix D: **Bitwise Examples in C**

This is the source code for a very simple C program to demonstrate some common bitwise operations in C.

```c
/* bitwise.c - examples of various bitwise operations (BFH)
 * Fri Apr  6 16:51:37 EDT 2018 BFH first version
 */

#include <stdio.h>
#include <unistd.h>

int main(int argc, char *argv[]) {
    int nums[] = {-1, 0, 2, 999};
    int i;

    // id self to user
    printf(
      "%s: work through some bitwise operator examples0,
      argv[0]);

    puts("0ogical And");
    printf("0 & 0...");
    if (0 & 0) {
        puts("true");
    } else {
        puts("false");
    }

    printf("1 & 1...");
    if (1 & 1) {
        puts("true");
    } else {
        puts("false");
    }

    printf("0 & 1...");
    if (0 & 1) {
        puts("true");
    } else {
        puts("false");
    }
```

```
     puts("Oogical Or");
     printf("0 | 0...");
     if (0 | 0) {
          puts("true");
     } else {
          puts("false");
     }

     printf("1 | 1...");
     if (1 | 1) {
          puts("true");
     } else {
          puts("false");
     }

     printf("1 | 0...");
     if (1 | 0) {
          puts("true");
     } else {
          puts("false");
     }

     puts("Oesting values to see if they are true");
     for (i = 0; nums[i] != 999; i++) {
          printf("%2d is...",nums[i]);
          puts( (nums[i])? "true" : "false" );
     }

     exit(0);
}

/* eof */
```

Appendix E: **Bit Flags Examples in C**

This is the source code for a very simple C program to demonstrate some common bit flag operations in C.

```c
/* bits.c - trying out various bitwise operations as examples (BFH
 * Fri Apr  6 16:51:37 EDT 2018 BFH first version
 */


#include <stdio.h>
#include <unistd.h>

#define ERR_DB   1
#define ERR_BLANK_NAME   2
#define ERR_NAME_NOT_FOUND       4
#define ERR_MULTI_MATCH 8

int main(int argc, char *argv[]) {
    char * pmask_name;
    int bit_flags = 0;
    int rv;
    int i;
    int mask;
    int masks[] = {ERR_DB,
                   ERR_BLANK_NAME,
                   ERR_NAME_NOT_FOUND,
                   ERR_MULTI_MATCH,
                   0};

    /* let us set each bit */
    puts("Setting all the flags...");
    for (i = 0; masks[i] != 0; i++) {
        mask = masks[i];

        // name the mask
        pmask_name = "UNKNOWN";
        if (mask == ERR_DB) pmask_name = "Database I/O";
        if (mask == ERR_BLANK_NAME) pmask_name = "Blank Name";
        if (mask == ERR_NAME_NOT_FOUND) pmask_name = "Name Not Found";
        if (mask == ERR_MULTI_MATCH) pmask_name = ">1 Names Matched";

        // set the flag
        bit_flags = (bit_flags | mask);
```

```c
        printf("mask=%d, bit_flags=%2d error=%s0,mask,bit_flags,pmask_name);
    }

    /* let us test each bit */
    puts("0esting all the flags...");
    for (i = 0; masks[i] != 0; i++) {
        mask = masks[i];

        // set the flag
        rv = (bit_flags & mask);

        printf("mask=%d, bit_flags=%d rv=%d0,mask,bit_flags,rv);
    }

    /* let us clear each bit */
    puts("0learing all the flags...");
    for (i = 0; masks[i] != 0; i++) {
        mask = masks[i];

        // clear the flag
        //bit_flags &= ~(1 << i);
        bit_flags &= ~(mask);

        printf("mask=%d, bit_flags=%d0,mask,bit_flags);
    }

    exit(0);
}

/* eof */
```

Appendix F: **Toy Encrypt / Decrypt**

This is the source code from the URL below, slightly tweaked.

```
http://c-program-example.com/2012/04/c-program-to-encrypt-and-
decrypt-a-password.html
```

```c
/*************************************************************
 * * You can use all the programs on  www.c-program-example.com
 * * for personal and learning purposes. For permissions to use the
 * * programs for commercial purposes,
 * * contact info@c-program-example.com
 * * To find more C programs, do visit www.c-program-example.com
 * * and browse!
 * *
 * *                          Happy Coding
 * ************************************************************/

/* tiny edits by Brendan Hemingway to clean up output */

#include <stdio.h>
#include <string.h>

void encrypt(char password[],int key)
{
    unsigned int i;
    for(i=0;i<strlen(password);++i)
    {
        password[i] = password[i] - key;
    }
}

void decrypt(char password[],int key)
{
    unsigned int i;
    for(i=0;i<strlen(password);++i)
    {
        password[i] = password[i] + key;
    }
}
char * BinDump(char password[])
{
    unsigned int i;
```

```
    for(i=0;i<strlen(password);++i)
    {
        printf("[%d]",(password[i]) & 127);
    }
    putchar('0);
}
int main()
{
    char password[20] ;
    printf("Enter a password: ");
    scanf("%s",password);
    printf("Input value    = %s0,password);
    encrypt(password,0xFACA);
    //printf("Encrypted value = %s0,password);
    printf("Encrypted value = "); BinDump(password);
    decrypt(password,0xFACA);
    printf("Decrypted value = %s0,password);
    return 0;
}
/* eof */
```

Appendix G: **Binary Search in Perl**

This is the source code for the binary search example.

```perl
# binsearch.pl - sample searching program (BFH)

# create the sorted haystack
my @sh = (qw/A B C D E F G H I J K L M N O P Q R S T U V W X Y Z/);
print join('',@sh),"0;

# create the unsorted haystack
my @uh = ();
foreach my $let (@sh) {
    # let us randomly assign a matrix index to this letter
    my $idx = rand(26);
    while (defined($uh[$idx])) {
        $idx = rand(26);
    }
    $uh[$idx] = $let;
}
print join('',@uh),"0;

#
# now find each element in both ways
#
my %a = ();
my %b = ();
for (my $x = 0; $x < @sh; $x++) {
    my $let = $sh[$x];

    # simple search
    for (my $i = 0; $i < @uh; $i++) {
        if ($let eq $uh[$i]) {
            $a{$let} = $i+1;
            last;
        }
    }

    # binary search
    my $flag = 1;
    my($start,$stop) = (0,scalar @sh);
    my $len = ($stop - $start);
    my $j = 0;
```

```perl
        while ($flag && $j < @sh) {
            # time for simple scan?
            if ($len < 5) {
                for (my $i = $start; $i <= $stop; $i++) {
                    ++$j;
                    if ($sh[$i] eq $let) {
                        $b{$let} = $j;
                        last;
                    }
                }
                $flag = 0;
                last;
            }

            # continue binary search
            my $idx = int($len / 2) + $start;
            my $rc = ($let cmp $sh[$idx]);

            ++$j;

            if ($rc == 0) {
                $b{$let} = $j;
                $flag = 0;
                last;
            } elsif ($rc < 0) {
                # start stays the same
                $stop = $idx;
            } elsif ($rc > 0) {
                $start = $idx;
                # stop stays the same
            }
            $len = ($stop - $start);
        }
    }


# check out the min / max / average
my($tot,$c) = (0,0);
my($min,$max,$avg) = (99,-1,0);
foreach my $let (keys %a) {
    my $j = $a{$let};
    if ($j < $min) {
        $min = $j;
    }
    if ($j > $max) {
```

```perl
            $max = $j;
        }
        $tot += $j;
        ++$c;
    }
    $avg = ($tot / $c);
    printf "Unsorted, simple search: %d/%d/%.2f min/max/avg0,$min,$max,$avg;

    # check out the min / max / average
    ($tot,$c) = (0,0);
    ($min,$max,$avg) = (99,-1,0);
    foreach my $let (keys %b) {
        my $j = $b{$let};
        if ($j < $min) {
            $min = $j;
        }
        if ($j > $max) {
            $max = $j;
        }
        $tot += $j;
        ++$c;
    }
    $avg = ($tot / $c);
    printf "sorted, binary search: %d/%d/%.2f min/max/avg0,$min,$max,$avg;
    exit(0);
    # eof
```

Index

A

Agile 99, 102, 103

API (Application Program Interface) 91, 108, 137, 138

Application Software (apps) 57, 95, 96, 101, 114, 117, 139, 147

B

Boole 28, 29, 34, 36, 67, 73, 78

Booting 51, 52, 53, 115

Bug 50, 60, 99, 149, 166, 172, 174, 175, 177, 178, 179, 180, 181

C

Client/Server 13, 168, 169, 170, 171

Cloud 18, 19, 167

Codd (father of relational databases) 143, 147, 148

CPU 21, 23, 24, 25, 26, 27, 31, 33, 34, 36, 41, 43, 44, 49, 51, 54, 56, 86, 98, 108, 109, 114, 134, 139, 140, 142, 151, 177, 188, 190

D

DBMS (Database Management System) 137, 138, 139, 140, 141, 142, 144, 145, 146, 170

debug 13, 21, 63, 91, 94, 97, 98, 99, 103, 104, 105, 169, 172, 173, 174, 175, 176, 177, 178, 179, 180, 181

Dynamic Link Library (DLL) 95, 96, 97

E

environment 21, 23, 37, 44, 45, 51, 54, 56, 73, 86, 87, 89, 90, 91, 93, 94, 95, 96, 97, 99, 101, 103, 104, 107, 112, 115, 118, 122, 125, 126, 127, 136, 147, 169, 175, 176, 178

F

Firmware 25

Flang 63, 64, 67

G

GUI 37, 117

H

HTML (Hyper Text Markup Language) 101, 105, 113, 142, 143

I

Intrinsics 94, 104

IP 159, 160, 161, 162, 163, 164, 165, 168, 171

L

LAN 161, 162, 163, 171

LHS (Left Hand Side) 71, 72

Linux 87, 111, 112, 118, 119, 121, 176

M

Mac 24, 26, 31, 36, 37, 38, 39, 40, 41, 42, 43, 44, 46, 47, 48, 49, 50, 51, 52, 53, 54, 55, 56, 57, 58, 61, 70, 81, 82, 86, 87, 88, 89, 90, 93, 94, 97, 98, 118, 119, 130, 131, 159, 160, 164, 166, 169, **195**

Machine Code 31, 97

www.ingramcontent.com/pod-product-compliance
Lightning Source LLC
Chambersburg PA
CBHW071114050326
40690CB00008B/1223